An Even Break

An Even Break

Sid Hite

HOUGHTON MIFFLIN BOSTON • MORRIS PLAINS, NJ
California • Colorado • Georgia • Illinois • New Jersey • Texas

For my nephews,
Aidan, Ian, Nolan, and Luke

Cover illustration by Mark Elliott

Houghton Mifflin Edition, 2001

Printed in the U.S.A.

ISBN: 0-618-05997-0

23456789-B-06 05 04 03 02 01 00

An Even Break

Chapter 1

Many folks in Wilma felt a bit sorry for Frisk Tilden and his mother, Shelly. There was nothing wrong with the pair—they weren't dumb or weird or odd or anything unspeakable. In fact, they were both rather likable individuals. The townspeople were concerned because Shelly was separated from her husband and Frisk had no father to raise him.

Shelly and Hank Tilden had dated during high school and gotten married soon after graduation. Hank worked as a plumber. Initially, the union was a happy affair. But then Hank began to spend more and more time out with his buddies, and Shelly's happiness faded. They argued for months, and then, three weeks before Frisk was born, Hank moved away from Wilma.

Since Frisk had never met his father, he didn't miss the man in a personal way. When he did think about him, Frisk just missed the idea of how things might have been different if Hank had stayed in Wilma. As far as the townspeople were concerned, Frisk didn't give a hoot whether they felt sorry for him and his mother or not. He was happy with the life they had together.

Frisk's real name was Francis, although no one except for his Aunt Rachel ever called him that. Rachel, who lived in Richmond, was Shelly's older sister. Ironically, it was Rachel who gave Frisk his nickname in the first place.

She gave him the name when he was two years old and in an extremely rambunctious phase of development. At the time, his actions were guided by a simple and driving desire to be wherever he was not. If he was placed on the floor, he wanted to climb on the couch. If he was on the couch, he felt an urgent need to get down on the floor. He didn't care where he went, as long as it was away from where he already was. He loved open doors, hallways, stairways, and any object that remotely resembled a ladder.

It was near the end of a weekend visit and Rachel was preparing to depart for Richmond. She shook her head, rolled her eyes, and said to Shelly, "Francis is a cute boy, but he's got to be the friskiest child I've ever seen. Shelly, you aren't feeding him jumping beans, are you?" Rachel sighed. "I'm worn-out just from watching him ramble around the living room."

"He does keep you hopping," said Shelly, and she meant it.

Now Frisk was twelve. He still had plenty of energy, but he was no longer the hyperactive blur of movement he had once been. The combination of a disciplined upbringing and the natural mellowing of age had slowed him down to an almost normal pace. In fact, these days he was something of a thinker, more inclined to observe his surroundings than to hurry around them. Even so, he was still called Frisk. Once established, nicknames are not easy to shake.

Frisk was four feet five inches tall, and skinny. He had large ears and a dimpled chin. Springing from his head was an unruly mass of red hair. His eyes were bright blue, he was speckled all over with freckles, and he had a high-pitched voice. Sometimes, much to his embarrassment, he squeaked when he got excited.

Frisk and Shelly lived in a four-room apartment in downtown Wilma. The apartment was located above Billy Compton's hardware store. If you could find the town, it was a cinch finding the store. Wilma had only one street.

As small towns go, Wilma was the kind of place where everyone pretty much knew everyone else. Usually that was a good thing, but sometimes it wasn't. Familiarity breeds gossip, and depending on who you were and what you had been up to lately, maybe you wouldn't want to know everyone. Yet the folks from Wilma were a forgiving crowd. Unless a person was actively trying to start trouble, they tended to accept people for who they were, even if that included a few minor foibles and quirks.

While we are speaking of the townspeople and their opinions, there was another reason they felt sorry for Frisk and Shelly: The boy and his mother were poor. This was not Shelly's fault. She worked as a clerk in a grocery store, where she had ambitions of becoming a manager, and she was extremely cautious about letting money leave her hand. Except for an occasional trip to the movies, she limited her expenditures to the basic necessities of life.

Even so, at the end of each month after Shelly had paid all the bills, there was rarely much money left over. If by chance there were a few dollars to spare, she took them straight to the local bank. As she explained to Frisk, "I'm saving the money so we'll be prepared in case of an emergency."

No doubt the money was available for emergencies, but Shelly had a secret. For many years she had been dreaming of buying a small house on the outskirts of Wilma, and in her heart this was what she was saving for. Although the apartment where she and Frisk lived was clean and safe, she didn't think of it as a proper home. She wanted a place where Frisk could run around in the open air and she could have a garden.

Frisk never complained about being poor. Complaining was just not his style. Although he was well aware of Shelly's secret (on numerous occasions he had overheard her on the telephone with Rachel, whispering about buying a house), he never let on that he knew. He wished there was something he could do to help his mom fulfill her dream, but he couldn't think of anything.

For months Frisk thought about how things stood at home and pondered ways he might improve the situation. Yet the subject was large, and the more he dwelled on the matter, the more perplexed he became.

As Frisk often did when he was perplexed, he turned to Pepper Parker for advice. Pepper was Frisk's fishing buddy. Like Frisk, Pepper was twelve. Unlike Frisk, Pepper was the opposite of skinny.

One warm day in March, Frisk and Pepper were sitting on the the bridge just south of Wilma. They had no fishing gear with them. They were soaking up the warmth, watching reflected clouds dance on the surface of the Turkey Scratch River. "You know, Pepper," Frisk said languidly, "I wish I had a bunch of money."

Pepper grinned and replied with an amused snort, "Don't we all?"

Frisk frowned. "Never mind. I'm not going to discuss it with you."

"Discuss what? You want a bunch of money?"

"Forget it, Pepper. Forget I ever mentioned it."

Pepper was silent for several minutes. He could see that Frisk's feeling were hurt about something. Finally, half as a joke and half just to say something, Pepper remarked, "I'm sure you've thought of this, Frisk, but if you want money, the best way to get it is to have a paying job."

Frisk shrugged solemnly. "I know that, Pepper. But where am I going to find a job in Wilma?"

"Probably nowhere," Pepper admitted. "I was just saying that's what you need."

"I mean, I'm only twelve. Who's gonna hire me?"

"Probably nobody."

There was another long moment of silence during which the boys watched the clouds play upon the river. The silence ended abruptly when Frisk jumped to his feet and declared, "That's it, Pepper. I don't care what it takes, but I'm going to find a job."

"Good luck," Pepper said meekly. He had grown up near Wilma, and he knew Frisk's chances of finding a job were slight. "Frisk, as a favor, can I ask you not to hold me responsible for giving you the idea?"

A smile broke over Frisk's determined face. "Sure," he said cheerfully, "but when I get a good job that pays lots of money, you'll be wanting credit for suggesting it."

For the next two months, every day except for Sunday when the town was mostly closed, Frisk pestered each and every shop owner in Wilma about giving him a job. He tried the gas station, the bank, the grocery store, the five-and-dime, the pharmacy, the hardware store, the movie theater, the luncheonette—he tried them all. Any job, that's all he was asking for. He didn't expect much. He knew that a skinny, twelve-year-old boy couldn't afford to be picky.

Chapter 2

Compton's Hardware was housed on the ground floor of a large, two-story wooden building that was over one hundred years old. Although the windows sagged toward the center, and the front porch slanted to the south, the structure was sturdy and in no risk of falling down. The outside was painted yellow. When it rained, the building looked like it was covered with splotches of mustard. And yet somehow the place appeared natural where it stood—as if it had grown up slowly on the spot.

The business belonged to Billy Compton. He had started working in the store when he was nine years old, and twenty-four years later he inherited the place from his father. Billy was a tall, broad-shouldered man with a quiet demeanor. He did enjoy a bit of polite joking now and then, but he was not the sort of fellow to tolerate any actual foolishness. Everyone around Wilma had a lot of respect for Billy.

The store offered everything from building

materials to electrical components, from hunting gear to garden supplies, from office equipment to kitchenware. At Compton's you could buy magazines, sporting goods, and radios; or shoes, work clothes, and tools.

Although Billy's inventory was extensive and varied, there was another feature to the store, which made the place especially attractive to the youngsters in Wilma. The appealing feature was in the rear of the store, located behind a black metal door. On the door was a sign that read Must Be Fifteen or Older to Enter. This was the entrance to Compton's Billiard Parlor, known locally as the Back Room. If you were an idle teenage boy it was where you wanted to be on a hot summer day. (It would have been the place to be on a winter day as well, but the parlor was only open from June through August. Billy was a firm believer in education and refused to do anything that might contribute to delinquency. No amount of argument could persuade him differently.)

There was nothing fancy about the Back Room. It was thirty feet square and paneled with plywood. It had plank flooring and two ventilation windows set near the top of the east wall. Beneath the windows was a fire exit. There was a clock on the wall above the exit. Naked lightbulbs dangled from black cords attached to open beams in the high ceiling.

The parlor sported three regulation-sized pool tables, two pinball machines, a refreshment booth, a rotating fan, and an old sofa. Rules were posted above the refreshment booth. They were all nos: No Credit. No Cursing. No Gambling. No Smoking. No Arguing with the Manager.

Because of the small size of the parlor and the many nos that were posted there, most older guys who wanted to shoot pool drove the seventeen miles to Ashland, where there was a large smoke-filled parlor with plenty of action. But for those teenagers still on foot, the nos were acceptable and Compton's was the place to be on a summer day. Indeed, it was such a desirable place to be that many thirteen- and fourteen-year-old boys spent a lot of time wishing they were older than they actually were. At least once a year some bold youngster would try to pretend he was fifteen and enter the restricted parlor. It was a mistake. Billy had both a watchful eye and an excellent memory for birthdays.

Although trouble was rare in the parlor, Billy installed a button in the refreshment booth that was connected to a buzzer in the hardware store. If events got out of hand and the Back Room manager decided he needed help, a push of the button would bring Billy running.

In all of Wilma there were two people who had keys to the black metal door leading into the Back

Room. One of these people, of course, was Billy Compton. The other person holding a key was the manager of the Back Room. The manager's position was coveted by just about every teenage boy in Wilma. Much to Pepper Parker's surprise and Frisk Tilden's delight, this was the job that Frisk secured for himself.

There was lots of grumbling when Frisk was hired to manage the Back Room. As far as the local teens were concerned, it was not fair that an underage kid should be given the position they all wanted. "He's a squirt."

"He looks like a scarecrow with measles."

"He only got hired because Billy felt sorry for his mother."

Of course, no one complained directly to Billy Compton. But Wilma being Wilma, Billy eventually received reports about the complaining. He just chuckled and explained: "I hired Frisk because he was as persistent as an aching tooth! He came in every day and begged for the job. The way I figure, anyone that determined deserves a chance to prove himself."

The parlor was open from eleven to six, Monday through Saturday. And six meant six o'clock sharp. Billy did not tolerate stragglers or excuses.

Opening day in the Back Room was an eye-opener for Frisk. He had not realized before that the game of pool was so serious, or that the players would be so passionate about their individual performances. There was an aura of sophistication that seemed to hover over the parlor and Frisk felt lucky just to be a part of the scene. As he informed Pepper at the end of his first day of employment, "It's a whole different world in the Back Room. Pool is the coolest game ever invented. I love working in there."

"In that case, I'm glad I suggested you get the job," Pepper said modestly.

"Right," Frisk laughed. "You're a genius."

Chapter 3

Frisk's first few weeks on the job were both difficult and exciting. Determined that Billy would never regret hiring him, he reported early for work each day, he kept scrupulous track of the money in the cash box, and he made sure that the floor and the trash can were spotless after closing time. Yet it was not these routine duties that caused problems. His difficulties lay in his relationship with the Back Room customers. As might have been expected, he did not receive a particularly warm welcome from the crowd of regulars who patronized the parlor. Basically, Frisk had three strikes against him: One, he was only twelve. Two, he had the job that others wanted. Three, he was as skinny as a stick. And these were just his basic faults. Other flaws were found and announced at random intervals.

Teddy Wald was Frisk's harshest critic. Teddy was seventeen and nearly twice the size of Frisk. He was volatile, and was feared by anyone his size or smaller. He seemed to find special joy in threatening to twist Frisk's ears. And on the day that Frisk dared to remind Teddy of the no-smoking rule, Teddy got so angry he struck the wall with his fist and bruised his knuckles.

Frisk was a bit nervous during his maiden weeks as the Back Room manager, but he was not daunted. He had a job to do and he did it. His enthusiasm for a regular income supplied him with much patience. As he explained to Pepper, patience was the best weapon against trouble. "The way I figure, it's less fun for the guys to pick on me if I don't let them know I'm bothered. And if they're not having fun, they'll get bored and stop."

"Yeah, maybe . . ." Pepper allowed, "but you don't want them to push you around all summer."

"No, I don't," Frisk agreed. "That's why I'm keeping quiet about the teasing. No one likes to hear complaining. I've got to win their respect."

"Hmmm." Pepper paused in thought, then broke into a laugh. "I wish I'd have been there when Teddy smashed his hand."

"It does seem funny now," Frisk said with a smile, "but at the time, I wasn't laughing."

Frisk's patience policy proved to be a wise policy. One by one the guys took note of his reserve, and then, bit by bit over a period of approximately three weeks, their criticisms of him grew less harsh. Soon, Frisk was an accepted feature in the Back Room. He was delighted. He still got teased on occasion, but then everyone got teased by someone at some point. He didn't take it personally. Only one thing really mattered—his job—and so far, so good. He'd made it through a difficult beginning.

Adding to Frisk's delight, on the last weekend in June he became friends with Dan Breedon. Dan was not only the best pool player for miles around, he was also one of the coolest guys in Wilma. He was dark-haired, handsome, and in his early thirties.

The friendship started that Saturday when Dan lingered in the parlor until closing time. At six o'clock Frisk shyly and reluctantly informed Dan that he had to lock up so he could sweep the floors. Yet Dan didn't take the hint and leave. Instead he surprised Frisk by remarking, "I've been watching you. I've got a hunch you might have the makings of a good pool player."

"Me?"

Dan laughed. "Yes. You seem to have an even temperament, and if you've got a good eye to go with it, that's all you need."

Frisk shrugged. He didn't know what to say.

"It's simple, Frisk: Shooting good pool is a lot like playing a musical instrument. First you learn the basics correctly, then you practice what you've learned. The rest is just a matter of concentration."

Frisk was wide-eyed with interest, but he still did not know what to say.

Dan nodded toward the middle table. "Rack 'em up and I'll give you a few pointers."

Frisk hesitated. "That's nice of you, Dan, but Billy said I have to close at six o'clock sharp. No exceptions."

Dan nodded again at the middle table. "I spoke with Billy earlier, and he said it was fine if I gave you lessons."

From that evening on, once or twice a week throughout the following month, Dan lingered in the parlor and instructed Frisk in the fundamentals of shooting pool. It was a private arrangement. None of the regular crowd had the slightest idea that Dan was giving Frisk lessons.

Besides teaching Frisk the rudiments of how to hold a cue stick properly, how to square his shoulders to the cue ball, and other such basics, Dan never failed to remind his student: "Concentrate. That's the key to good shooting."

Concentrate Frisk did, whether Dan was there to coach him or not. After his first experience of knocking a colored object ball into a pocket he fell utterly in love with the game of pool. During the day while he watched the others playing, he could hardly wait for evenings so he could practice. He loved the feel of the green felt. He loved the weight of a cue stick in his hands. He loved the sound of the balls clacking together. He loved the feeling he got when an object ball disappeared into the pocket where he had aimed it. Dan had been right, Frisk did have the makings of a good player.

Pepper Parker had been happy for Frisk when he found his job, yet there was a part of him that had felt left out. Like most underage boys in Wilma, he was intrigued by the Back Room. And now, listening to his own best friend talk about the thrill of shooting pool, Pepper felt downright envious. "Gosh, Frisk, it sounds more exciting than hooking a big bass."

"It might not be more exciting than hooking a bass," Frisk replied honestly, "but it's gobs of fun. I don't know if I can explain it or not. It's . . . well, you know how when you cast a lure on the river and it lands exactly where you wanted it to land—you know the feeling you get?"

"Yeah, I know the feeling."

"Well it's a lot like that . . . like you've done something just right. Only pool is played inside, and instead of catching a fish you knock a ball into a pocket."

Pepper looked blankly at Frisk.

Frisk shrugged apologetically. "Sorry, I knew I wouldn't be able to explain it."

Pepper shook his head. "I can't believe you actually get paid to hang around in the Back Room. That's like me getting paid to sit by the river."

"Just think," Frisk said with quick laugh. "If you hadn't have talked me into getting a job, we'd both be sitting by the river and neither one of us would have any money."

"Thanks for reminding me," Pepper growled. "And speaking of the river, we haven't gone fishing together for two weeks."

Frisk smiled at his old pal. "Tomorrow, Pepper. Tomorrow is Sunday. I'll meet you on the bridge at noon."

Chapter 4

Pepper and Frisk went fishing three times in July, always on a Sunday when Frisk was not working. Pepper wasn't happy about his friend's busy schedule, but he understood and didn't whine about his loss of a fishing partner.

During the same period, Frisk received five pool lessons from Dan Breedon. These lessons, along with the many hours that Frisk practiced alone, soon began to show definite results. Toward the end of the month it was evident that Frisk had begun to develop a certain knack for the game. After the fifth and final lesson in July, Dan paid him the ultimate compliment. "You made some fine shots this evening. I'm not sure if I have anything else to teach you."

Frisk blushed modestly. "Well . . . I do try to concentrate."

Dan set his cue stick in the wall rack. "So, how are things at home? Shelly doing okay?"

"She's fine. She works a lot, but she's fine."

"I saw her yesterday at the store," Dan said casually. "Tell her I said hello, will ya?"

"Sure, Dan. I'll tell her. No problem."

On the first Saturday in the hot, humid month of August, promptly at a quarter to eleven, Frisk reported to work at the hardware store. As usual, he was wearing a clean T-shirt tucked neatly into a pair of jeans and his red hair was brushed almost into submission.

"Morning, Frisk," Billy said as he handed the cash box across the counter. "The change is all counted out. I'll check with you later to see if you need more quarters."

"Thanks." Frisk nestled the box under an arm. "So, I reckon we'll be jumping today."

"Always are on Saturday," Billy noted.

Frisk blushed. "I meant, you know . . . with the tournament coming and everything. The guys will be wanting extra practice. We might be busier than usual."

Billy nodded. "I see what you mean."

Each year at the end of August, Billy Compton sponsored the Wilma Eight Ball Tournament. It was a popular event that raised one hundred and fifty dollars for the Patrick Henry Library at the north end of Wilma. The winner of the tournament received one hundred dollars and the runner-up took home fifty. It was open to the first twenty players that paid the entry fee of fifteen dollars.

"Have many people signed up yet?" asked Frisk.

"Almost full," said Billy, turning to gaze out the window. "I see Teddy Wald and some of his buddies leaning against the bank. I guess they're anxious to get started."

Frisk frowned at the mention of Teddy's name.

Billy knew that Teddy Wald and some of the other fellows occasionally picked on his young manager, but since Frisk never complained about the matter, Billy chose not to mention it either. Instead, as he did each day before Frisk opened the parlor, he reminded the skinny redhead, "Don't forget to push the buzzer button if you need me."

"I won't forget." Frisk wished Billy would quit reminding him about the button. It was a source of certain pride for him that he had never needed to buzz for help. Of course, everyone knew that Billy Compton was never far away, and that knowledge did much to inspire good behavior in the Back Room patrons.

It was ten to eleven when Frisk unlocked the black metal door and entered the darkened room. He locked the door behind him and took the cash box to its keeping place in the refreshment booth. He flicked on the lights, plugged in the pinball machines, turned on the fan, and began putting the multicolored pool balls on the green tabletops.

Arranging the balls for the start of each game—

racking the table, as the task was called—was a service Frisk provided for his customers. Sometimes he received tips for this service.

At four minutes to eleven Frisk sat down on the old sofa to wait for opening time. While he waited, he recalled the busy Saturday in June when he received two dollars and ninety cents in tips. That was more than twice his usual take.

Two dollars and ninety cents, Frisk reflected. Not bad for a twelve-year-old kid from Wilma. Actually, it was pretty darn good when one considered that his tips came over and above a weekly salary of twelve dollars and fifty cents.

Frisk, having gone from nothing to an income of roughly fifteen dollars a week, had never quite gotten used to having money. Like his mother, he was exceptionally careful with every dollar he spent. From time to time he did buy a fishing lure to add to his collection, and when he went to the movies with Shelly he insisted on paying for his own ticket, but otherwise he was reluctant to part with his cash. Indeed, he was so concerned with holding on to his money, that he (again, like his mother), opened a savings account at the local bank. In his case though, it was a well-kept secret.

Frisk was hoping to have two hundred dollars saved by the end of summer. He did not know what he would do with that sum when he reached his goal—if he reached it—but he did enjoy considering his options. It was fun, thinking of all the things that money could buy. A canoe. A bicycle. Maybe a camera. He had even entertained the idea of giving the money to Shelly as part of a downpayment on her dream house.

So far Frisk had deposited one hundred and nine dollars in his account. Unfortunately, today was the third of August and it was looking as though he would fall short of his goal.

Frisk quit thinking about money and glanced at the clock on the wall above the refreshment booth. The long hand was pointing to twelve and the short hand was pointing to eleven. He got up, patted his hair, and went to unlock the black metal door.

It was opening time.

Chapter 5

By noon on that first Saturday in August the Back Room was already buzzing with activity. On the number-one table near the refreshment booth, Ellard Castle and Bingo Todd were shooting their third game of the day. On the number-three table at the other end of the parlor, Teddy Wald was preparing to play against Jason Farber. In the northeast corner Winky Nelson was hunched over the Surfrider pinball machine. He was trying to top Vernon Beazely's score of nine thousand points.

Frisk was racking the table for Teddy and Jason. As he lifted the rack from the pile he saw the white cue ball speeding in his direction. He snatched the wooden rack from the colorful pile and jumped backwards.

Whack! The cue ball plowed into the orderly arrangement and scattered the fifteen object balls around the table. An orange five ball fell into a side pocket.

Frisk glared at Teddy. He was thinking, *You should have your head examined!*

"Just wanted to see how fast you could move," Teddy said with a menacing snicker.

Frisk wondered what made Teddy tick. Some of the other guys were tough and argumentative, but at least they had clear boundaries and it was possible to reason with them. With Teddy, though, the boundaries were invisible and Frisk never knew whether he was trespassing or not. No one did. It was as if Teddy went out of his way to look for trouble.

Frisk continued to glare, but he did not say a word. If Teddy wanted to act like a jerk, that was his prerogative. Frisk wasn't going to goad him on by talking back.

Teddy turned to his friends to share a laugh, but they were not amused by his actions. Art Blatt rolled his eyes and shook his head in a negative manner. Jason Farber frowned and looked at the floor. Art and Jason liked Frisk. They knew he could have been hurt if the cue ball had hit his hands.

Teddy huffed, as if to suggest that no one could take a good joke anymore, and bent over the table to line up the seven ball. It should have been an easy shot, but when Teddy pushed the cue stick forward it wobbled in his hands, and the cue ball veered wide of its target.

Frisk chuckled beneath his breath.

"What are you laughing at?" Teddy took a threatening step toward Frisk. "Don't tell me you think you could have done better."

Yes, thought Frisk, *I could have done better. And if you knew how to concentrate you could have done better yourself.*

"Ah, leave him alone," Art said to Teddy. "You're just mad because you blew an easy shot."

Teddy ignored Art and addressed Frisk in an angry tone. "You think you're a big shot just because you work here. Well, you aren't. You're just a freckle-faced squirt. What do you know about shooting pool?"

Frisk crossed his arms and did his best to look fierce. He figured that one day, for better or worse, he was going to have to stand up to Teddy. Pepper was right; he couldn't let the guys push him around all summer. If today was the day, Frisk thought, then they might as well get it over with now.

Teddy rested his cue stick against the table and took another step forward. Frisk did not retreat. He prepared himself mentally. If Teddy made a move to swing at him, he was planning to fake to his right, then dip quickly to his left and smack the oaf on the head with the rack. The rack was made of solid oak. Frisk reckoned it would send a clear message.

Just at that moment the black metal door swung open and Dan Breedon strolled into the parlor. He surveyed the room with a glance, then nodded to Frisk. "How's it going?"

"Just dandy, Dan." Frisk's voice squeaked with relief. He knew he would have no more trouble from Teddy now that Dan was there.

Dan stared at Teddy. "You're not making trouble, are you?"

"No," said Teddy. He was cocky and rash, but he was not foolish enough to challenge Dan.

After Teddy returned to his game, Dan nodded to Frisk. "Rack up the center table, will ya? I've got an hour before I go on duty at the station."

The tension in the room dissipated and the parlor began to buzz with renewed activity. While pool balls clacked on all three tables and the pinball machines binged and pinged, Frisk moved constantly about the room, tending to his managerial duties. If he wasn't racking a table or collecting a game fee from one of the players, he was in the refreshment booth selling someone a bag of peanuts or a soda.

Of the numerous games that can be played on a pool table, eight ball was the most popular in Compton's Billiard Parlor. It was also the game featured in the annual tournament.

Eight ball has its detractors; there are people who say that an ability to play pool well is an indication of a misspent youth. Granted, eight ball has done little to increase the gross national product of America, yet it is a nonviolent pastime that requires sustained concentration; the playing of the game has soothed many a troubled mind. One might also argue that eight ball expands a player's attention span. Let the critics say what they will. Anyone who has played the game knows its rewards.

Not surprisingly, a crowd gathered to watch Dan practice on the middle table. Dan earned his living as a sheet-metal mechanic and was the captain of the Wilma Volunteer Fire Department, yet he was best known in the Back Room as a pool player. He had won the tournament for the past three years. Most reasonable people expected him to win again this year.

While Dan practiced, Frisk watched the crowd watching Dan and mused about something he had recently noticed. During the past month or so it seemed that his mother had asked about Dan several times a week. She was always casual with her inquiries, as if she was only moderately curious about the answer. But then a few days would pass and she would ask again. "So, how's Dan? Is he doing all right?" At the same time Frisk had noticed that Dan seemed equally curious about Shelly. He was also casual with his inquiries, maybe even more so than Shelly.

Frisk had initially been confused about whether there was any significance to what he'd noticed, or if it was all just a meaningless coincidence. But after discussing the matter with his rotund fishing partner, he'd been persuaded that something definite was in the air. Pepper had laughed when Frisk gave him the facts. "What's the mystery? It's obvious they're attracted to each other."

"You think Dan likes my mom, and she likes him?" Frisk was astonished by the concept. "I mean really, Pepper. My mom is an old woman. She's over thirty."

"Don't be so dense. Your mom isn't so old. At least not to Dan. He's an old guy too."

"Hmmm." Frisk pondered this for a moment. "Maybe you're right."

Pepper rocked with laughter. "Of course I'm right. Old people have feelings too."

By the time Dan put his cue stick in the wall rack, Frisk had begun to hatch a plot for getting Dan and Shelly in the same place at the same time.

"How much do I owe you?" Dan reached for his wallet.

"How many racks did you shoot?"

"Six."

Frisk calculated quickly. "That's a dollar and fifty cents. Say, Dan, have you seen *Doctor Zhivago*?"

"I have." Dan gave Frisk two dollars. "I saw it a couple of years ago when it played in town. Why do you ask?"

Frisk handed Dan his change. "Well, I'm supposed to see the movie with my mom tomorrow night. I was just curious if it was any good."

"It's a long movie," Dan noted, "but I liked it."

Frisk nodded thoughtfully. "Well, it must be pretty good. Mom has seen it twice already and she wants to see it again. I think we're going to the seven o'clock show."

Dan paused for an instant, then glanced at the two quarters Frisk had given him. He tossed them on the counter. "Those are for you. Thanks for racking. I gotta go."

"Thanks," Frisk said as Dan turned to depart. He wasn't sure if the lanky bachelor had gotten the hint or not.

Chapter 6

Frisk was tired at the end of that busy Saturday, but he was happy. After sweeping the floors and putting the trash can by the door, he dumped the contents of his hip pockets onto the middle table. It was time to count his tips.

Except for the two quarters Dan had given him, the pile of change consisted of dimes and nickels. Frisk counted carefully. The final tally was two dollars and five cents. It was far from a fortune, yet it was more than he had started the day with.

He gathered up his tips and grabbed the cash box from the refreshment booth. After a look around the parlor, he turned off the lights and exited through the black door. He drew the door tight, then double-checked to be sure it was properly locked.

Supper was on the table when Frisk got home. After dinner he and Shelly spent a quiet evening together. While she sat with a novel she had gotten from the library, he flipped through a back issue of

Sportsman magazine that Billy had given him. Later, when Shelly started humming the theme song from *Doctor Zhivago,* Frisk was reminded of the plot he had hatched earlier in the day.

Frisk slept late on Sunday morning, dragging himself out of bed only when he heard bacon sizzling in the kitchen. Sunday was his favorite day of the week. Neither he nor Shelly worked on Sundays. Sometimes they went to church, but usually not. Either way, she always made it a point to fix a big breakfast.

Frisk ate two eggs, two strips of bacon, and one slice of buttered toast smothered with honey. After washing it all down with a glass of orange juice, he told Shelly, "Pepper and I are going fishing today. I'm meeting him on the bridge at noon."

Shelly removed the dishes from the table and set them in the sink. "Looks like a nice day for getting out," she acknowledged. "But don't forget, we've got a date for the movies this evening. I want to see the matinee at four-thirty, so get home with plenty of time to take a shower before we go."

Frisk's jaw tightened. He had told Dan they were going to the seven o'clock show. They would miss him if they went to the matinee. Thinking as fast as he could, Frisk began to fabricate an excuse for being late. "Gee, Mom, I don't know if I can make it back by four-thirty. I'll try, but Pepper and I were planning to fish down the banks to Sparta."

"Sparta!" exclaimed Shelly. Sparta was a small

town eight miles south of Wilma. It was a long way for a twelve-year-old boy to wander. "Do Pepper's parents know you're planning to walk to Sparta?"

"Yes," said Frisk. He didn't enjoy misleading Shelly, but when there was a good reason for doing so—like now—he was capable of fudging the truth. "Please, Mom. I promised Pepper I'd go with him."

Shelly gave Frisk a long look. Frisk knew it well; it meant she needed more convincing.

"Mom . . . it wouldn't matter if it was just me," Frisk said in a suddenly sincere and thoughtful manner. "But Pepper has been feeling bad lately. He thinks I've abandoned him. If I don't go with him, he'll be hurt . . . maybe even depressed. You don't want to be responsible for Pepper getting depressed, do you?"

Shelly sighed. When Frisk really wanted to do something, he could be quite persuasive. "Okay. Go ahead. But be careful."

The Turkey Scratch River is a lazy little movement of water that meanders indecisively through the range of swampy woodlands lying between the small towns of Wilma and Sparta. The banks along this stretch of the river are rife with mud flats, sandbars, vine-filled ravines, thick reeds and grasses, and innumerable fallen, rotten trees. To say the least, it isn't an easy stroll.

By two-thirty the boys had caught four fish between them and had traveled less than halfway to Sparta. (Since none of the fish were bragging size, they were returned to the water.) It was at this point that Pepper announced it was time for him to head back. "I told Mom I'd be home by three," he explained.

Frisk didn't try to delay his friend. He knew Pepper's parents were strict about time. From where they stood at the moment, it was already likely that Pepper was going to be late.

The boys said little to each other as they followed the riverbank back toward Wilma. When they reached the bridge Frisk shook Pepper's hand, said a quick good-bye, then ducked under the rusty metal span.

"Why are you going under there?" asked Pepper.

"I'm hiding."

"From what?"

"From four-thirty."

Pepper laughed. "You can't hide from time."

"Yes I can," Frisk called from the shadows. "Now go on home before you're really late."

Pepper scrambled up the riverbank and started across the bridge. When he was halfway he stopped to lean over the railing and holler, "Hey, Frisk, be careful. There's a pool down there that's full of leeches. I got 'em all over me last time I went under the bridge."

Chapter 7

Although no leeches were attached to Frisk when he emerged from under the bridge at about five o'clock, he had been adopted by a rather ambitious odor. It followed him back to the apartment where Shelly waited impatiently. She greeted him with a wrinkled nose and dispatched him directly to the shower.

Shelly stayed mad at Frisk until a quarter to seven. They were standing in line to buy their tickets when her mood changed. Frisk knew he'd been forgiven because he could hear her humming the theme song from the movie they were about to see.

They were next in line at the window when Frisk saw Dan drive by in his Chevrolet Impala. It looked at first as if Dan intended to keep driving, but then the Impala made a quick U-turn in the street and glided into a parking spot across from the theater.

Frisk and Shelly were in the lobby admiring the

coming-attractions posters when Dan approached and bid them a somewhat sheepish hello.

"Howdy, Dan," Frisk saluted.

"Hi," Shelly said smiling.

Frisk was alarmed by the strange expression on Dan's face. He seemed edgy about something. One of his cheeks appeared to have a cramp, and his lips were drawn firmly in a straight line. After staring rather intently at Shelly, he whirled around and began to study the *Doctor Zhivago* poster. Then his head turned and his mouth opened. Frisk and Shelly thought he was going to speak, but Dan didn't say a word. He turned back to the poster.

Shelly attempted to break the ice. "It's my favorite movie," she said with a trill in her voice. "I saw it when it first came out. Then I saw it two years ago when it came back to Wilma."

Dan's eyes stayed glued to the poster.

Shelly tried again. "Have you seen it before, Dan?"

Dan turned. He seemed much more steady. "I saw it the last time it was here. And I liked it too."

Shelly smiled. "I especially love the music."

"Oh yeah, the music is good," Dan agreed. "But me, I'm partial to the scenery. All that open space . . ."

"I hope there's lots of action," Frisk suddenly interjected. Neither Shelly nor Dan seemed interested in his remark.

Shelly said excitedly to Dan, "My favorite scene is when the horsemen are riding through the forest in the snow. Remember the sound of their hooves pounding?"

Suddenly, Dan seemed edgy again. Evidently he had forgotten the horses. Without giving any indication that he was about to do so, he dropped to one knee and began fiddling with a shoelace. (Frisk was baffled; the shoe looked fine to him.) Then, in a flash, Dan was standing again. "Say, Shelly. Mind if I sit with you and Frisk?"

"That would be nice," Shelly answered with a warm smile.

Dan turned to Frisk. "That okay with you?"

"Sure," Frisk said earnestly. "If there're three of us, we can get a giant-size box of popcorn."

Dan smiled. He seemed to be his old self again. "Giant size is good, Frisk, as long as it's my treat."

Dan purchased a large box of popcorn and handed it to Frisk, then Shelly led the trio to the front of the theater and pointed to seats in the center section. After some confusion about who should enter the row first, Shelly started toward the desired seats. Frisk followed. Dan was behind him. When they were settled in their seats, Frisk reasoned, "I guess I'll hold the popcorn. Dan, if you were in the middle, you'd hold it."

"Makes sense to me," Dan whispered.

"Help yourself."

"Thanks."

"Mom, if you want some popcorn, just reach over and get it."

"Shhh."

Frisk tried to enjoy the movie, but the characters were too serious, and the plot was so complicated that even the actors seemed lost. One of them was a poet, and Frisk just didn't go in for that sort of thing. An hour into the flick he fell asleep.

Frisk didn't wake up until near the end of the movie. When he looked at the screen, he saw an old man riding on a trolley car. It was an older version of the poet. He was looking out the window. Suddenly he recognized a woman walking down the sidewalk and he got very excited. He stood and began pushing past the other passengers toward the exit.

On his left, Frisk heard his mother making sniffling sounds. He turned and saw that her eyes were wet with tears. When he looked back at the screen, the poet had gotten off the trolley and was hurrying to catch up with the woman on the sidewalk. She didn't even know he was there. After a few steps the old man clutched at his tie, staggered forward, then spun around once and fell. Apparently he was having a heart attack. A crowd quickly gathered around him. Meanwhile, the woman kept walking.

Weird, Frisk thought. Why make a movie that ended unhappily?

He turned to his right. Dan's eyes were dry, yet he looked as if he'd been fighting to keep them that way.

There was a little more talking, and then the credits started to roll. Soon the houselights came up. Neither Shelly nor Dan moved until after the screen went blank. Frisk just couldn't figure it out: Why did people pay good money to go see sad movies? It seemed like such a waste.

When Frisk rose from his seat he noticed that the popcorn in his lap had hardly been touched.

As they left the theater Dan offered to give Frisk and Shelly a ride home.

"That's sweet," Shelly said with a giggle, "but the store is less than two hundred yards from here. I believe we'll walk. If you'd like to join us, please do."

Dan hesitated uncertainly.

"Aw come on and walk with us," urged Frisk.

That seemed to be all the encouragement Dan needed. "Okay."

Four minutes later the trio had arrived at the door to the stairway leading up to the Tildens' apartment. Dan, who had been silent during the walk through town, suddenly blurted, "That was a great movie. It was fun sitting with the two of you."

"Thanks again for the popcorn." Frisk yawned. He was ready for bed.

"It was a pleasure, Dan," Shelly said. "Perhaps we could see something else sometime."

"Sure," Dan replied enthusiastically. "Anytime."

"Good. I'll look forward to it." Shelly smiled. "Good night."

"Good night."

" 'Night," added Frisk.

When Shelly and Frisk were near the top of the stairs she sighed and remarked, "Dan Breedon is a bona fide gentleman."

"Yeah," Frisk agreed sleepily. "He's a pretty good guy."

Chapter 8

As the dog days of August crept slowly by and the date of the Wilma Eight Ball Tournament drew nearer, Compton's Billiard Parlor stayed so busy that weekdays seemed like Saturdays and Saturdays seemed like . . . well, busy Saturdays. Busy was fine with Frisk. The increased activity upped his daily tip average without generating too much extra work. He had to move faster than usual, but except for a minor dispute with Ellard Castle and a perpetual hounding from Teddy Wald, his job went as smoothly as could be expected.

Frisk's dispute with Ellard involved the number of games Ellard had played one day. Ellard claimed he only owed for five games, while Frisk argued that the correct number was seven. Initially, neither of them was willing to concede that they might have counted wrong, but after discussing the matter with Billy Compton, they reached a peaceful compromise. Frisk admitted that mistakes were made. And Ellard agreed to pay for six games.

With Teddy, however, there was no compromise. No matter what Frisk did or did not do, Teddy persisted in directing a stream of ill will at Frisk.

During the two months that Frisk had been working in the parlor he'd begun to develop a theory. The theory—actually, it was more of an insight—was built upon the premise that there were two types of people in the world. Type ones occasionally paused to think about things, then shaped their personalities to fit their thoughts. Type twos never thought about anything, thus allowing their personalities to shape them. Teddy Wald was definitely a type two.

Frisk, being a type one, thought deeply about the matter, and eventually he concluded that Teddy's irritable disposition stemmed from a pool of pain that existed inside of him. (Anyone who looked closely could see the pain in Teddy's eyes.) Rather than pause to think about his feelings and perhaps remedy his behavior, Teddy simply reacted to his own suffering. And when he reacted, he bullied the world around him.

Although Frisk had this theory, it didn't mean he was willing to forgive Teddy for being a jerk. All it meant was that Frisk had a better understanding of the situation and was thereby better able to deal with the annoyance. To a certain extent he felt sorry for the guy—but only to a certain extent. His basic instinct was to avoid Teddy whenever possible. Unfortunately, Wilma being the small town it was, and Frisk having the job he had, Teddy wasn't very easy to avoid.

In spite of the conflict with Teddy, August was a good month for Frisk. His relations with the regular crowd continued to improve, his savings account continued to grow, and he remained thrilled with his job. Also, he was steadily getting better with a cue stick. Since Shelly worked until seven-thirty on weekdays during August, Frisk was free to linger in the parlor for more than an hour each evening. The time was spent practicing the basics that Dan had taught him.

One of Dan's fundamental rules was to square your shoulders to the cue ball when lining up a shot. Yet Frisk had struggled with this since his first lesson. He was shorter than the average pool player and often couldn't reach the cue ball. Then one evening when he was stretching on his toes and trying to lean across the table, he suddenly perceived a solution to the problem. It was such a simple and obvious solution, he couldn't imagine why he hadn't thought of it before. He propped his cue stick against the table, marched over to the refreshment booth, grabbed a wooden crate, emptied it of soda bottles, then hauled the container to the table and stood upon it.

Eureka! All he had ever needed was a platform.

Now he could easily square his shoulders to the cue ball. Now he could really concentrate on his shots.

Frisk was eager to show the crate trick to Dan and to demonstrate his rapidly improving skill on the table, but much to Frisk's daily disappointment, Dan didn't give him a chance to show him anything. As it happened, Dan didn't appear in the parlor from the third of August until the final day of the month. Frisk began to worry that Dan was mad at him for some reason, or that Dan was having some kind of personal trouble. Then, in the third week of August, he learned from his mother that Dan was working lots of overtime at his job and simply didn't have time for pool. She had seen him in the grocery store. "He told me to be sure to give you his regards," Shelly cheerfully informed Frisk.

"That explains things," Frisk replied, then asked, "Mom, what are you smiling about?"

"Me? Am I smiling?"

"You're smiling," Frisk confirmed, "and it looks like you're hiding something."

"I'm not hiding anything . . . although Dan did ask me to the matinee on Sunday. *A Face in the Crowd* is playing."

"You going?"

"I told him I would. You can join us if you wish. Or if you prefer, you can go fishing and stay until suppertime."

Frisk could take a hint. "Fishing. No question."

. . .

Meanwhile, in the evenings, Frisk didn't let his lack of a teacher distract him from practicing. Instead, as he squared his shoulders and eyed his shots, he pretended that Dan was in the shadows watching him drive the cue stick forward. Frisk had an active imagination, and sometimes when he was taking aim at an object ball he could almost hear Dan's encouraging voice. *Now don't forget, concentration is the key to good shooting.*

By Saturday the twenty-fourth of August, one week before the tournament, the mood of anticipation in the parlor had grown to the point where one could see the dreams etched in the faces of the Back Room regulars. The fifteen-dollar entry fee was no small matter for any of the hopefuls, and though some of them joked about making charitable donations to the library, each entrant had serious designs on the hundred-dollar first prize. Many of the regulars were inspired by Dan's extended absence from the parlor. They reasoned hopefully that he'd be rusty on the big day.

As will happen when many people are anticipating the same event, there was avid and varied speculation about the outcome of the tournament. Predictions of an upset were plentiful, and there was a rich supply of wild rumors. One rumor that caused quite a stir was disseminated by Winky Nelson. He claimed that a pool shark from Richmond had mailed in the entry fee and was planning to drive to Wilma on the big day for some easy pluckings. Winky defended the rumor for two days, insisting that he had positive proof of the shark's intentions. He only admitted it was a joke after Art Blatt asked Billy Compton about the shark. "Baloney," said Billy.

Chapter 9

Frisk was the first customer through the door of the local bank on Monday morning. In his pocket was the forty-seven dollars he'd saved since his last deposit. He planned to spend two of these dollars on a fishing lure. The rest was for his account. After depositing the cash, and adding the dollar seventy cents in interest that he had been pleased to discover, Frisk had one hundred fifty-five dollars and seventy cents in the bank.

Although it was now almost certain that Frisk would not attain his original goal of two hundred dollars by the end of summer, he was still proud of his achievement. After all, one hundred and fifty-five smackeroos was a fair pile of dough.

Frisk was still considering ways to spend his money. Twice he had gone to inspect the fiberglass canoe that Jimmy Gray was trying to sell for a hundred dollars. Frisk wanted to buy it, but he had not even made an offer. It was a practical decision. There wasn't enough room in the apartment to keep a twelve-foot canoe.

Later that morning, when the Back Room got busy, Frisk wasn't surprised. He'd been expecting the regulars to appear. Most of them only had part-time jobs at best, and of those who were fully employed, many had arranged to take the week off. Others came in during their lunch break or at the end of an early day.

Although not surprised by the turnout, Frisk had not anticipated how intense everyone would be. The regulars were usually a gregarious lot, full of spunk and playful chatter, but today they came as independent operators who had little to say to each other. The sporting mood of the previous week had given way to silent tension. Rumor-mongering and speculation were out. It was time to practice. Except for Dan Breedon, who was working, and Winky Nelson, who had been keeping a low profile since his pool-shark story was exposed as baloney, all the regulars put in at least an hour apiece on one of the available tables.

The mood in the Back Room remained tense on Tuesday and Wednesday, and didn't shift until Thursday when Billy tacked the tournament roster on the wall. With the names of the entrants posted for all to see, the regulars were suddenly drawn from their ruminations and propelled into the arena of public debate. Almost as if the mood shift had been scheduled, the pundits were now compelled to speak.

A semicircle of pool players watched as Jason

Farber ran his finger down the roster. "You can forget that name, that name, this name, and those two there."

"You missed your name," noted Clayton Burns.

"I'm pointing at names to forget," retorted Jason.

"You can forget all the names, except for Dan Breedon," Art Blatt stated in a knowing tone. "He's the one to watch. I hope I don't draw him in an early round."

"Dan's probably going to be rusty," observed Clayton.

"I don't buy that theory," declared Art. "Dan has been shooting pool since before most of us were born. He's not going to rust up that quickly. Even if he does, I still wouldn't bet against him."

"Say, who's M. Todd?" Ellard Castle asked no one in particular.

Tim Reed replied. "That's Bingo Todd. His real name is Marion, but he doesn't like people to know that."

Ellard chuckled. "I wouldn't either if my name was Marion. Anyway, you can write Bingo off the list. He's all slop."

"If you can't shoot good, shoot hard."

"Anybody know a B. Ferris?" Art Blatt pointed at the roster.

"Nope."

"Never heard of him."

"Hey Frisk," Art called across the room. "Who is B. Ferris?"

Frisk thought for a second. "I don't know, unless Blanton Ferris has signed up to play."

"You mean the bank president? Mr. Ferris? No way."

"Maybe it's the shark from Richmond," suggested Tim. "Maybe Winky was telling the truth."

Art shrugged. "I doubt it. Anyway, whoever B. Ferris is, I'm not worried about him. Dan Breedon is my concern."

Ellard put an arm around Art and laughed heartily. "And we all know that right now Dan Breedon is hiding in a corner somewhere, biting his nails and saying to himself, 'I sure hope I don't have to play against Art Blatt. Please, please, not me.' "

After closing the Back Room at six o'clock that Thursday, Frisk hurried home to grab his fishing gear. There were two hours left before darkness and he was eager to try out the lure he'd recently purchased. It was a Mepps Silver Spinner. He figured it would work well in the fading light.

Shelly frowned when Frisk told her he'd be back by dark. "It's my one weeknight off from work, Frisk, and I just put a chicken in the oven. It's coming out in twenty minutes."

"Can you stall it?" asked Frisk.

"About as easily as you can stall your fishing."

With exaggerated piety, Frisk went to where Shelly was sitting and got down on his knees.

"Please, Mom. I just got a new lure this morning and I wanted to try it out."

Shelly sighed wearily. It was times like this when she regretted that Frisk had no father to fish with. "It worries me when you go out in the evenings."

Frisk rolled his eyes. "What's to worry about? Mom, tell me one thing to worry about."

"Frisk—" Shelly started to say something, then decided to keep the thought. After a long pause she said, "Okay, I'll hold supper. But take an apple with you and be back by eight."

There was a marvelous sunset in the making as Frisk stood on the bridge and cast his line into the Turkey Scratch. He'd been there for about twenty minutes when he saw something to worry about. Actually, it was not something, it was someone. It was Teddy Wald, walking directly toward the bridge.

As the muscles in Frisk's stomach tightened, he dismissed the option of running. In the back of his mind he'd been expecting this moment all summer. Now that it had arrived, he figured he might as well see it through.

Teddy lumbered up to where Frisk was standing and leaned forward against the railing. "Hey, Squirt. Had any luck?"

"One strike earlier. I think it was a pickerel."

"You mean a pike?"

"Yeah." Frisk nodded. Not knowing what else to do, he threw out his line again.

Teddy let a drop of spittle fall from his lips. It hit the water with a soft splat. "Lots of pike in this river."

"Yeah." Frisk cranked evenly on the reel.

"Big tournament tomorrow, huh?"

"Finally," said Frisk. He wasn't sure if he was reading the moment correctly, but it almost seemed as if Teddy was trying to be friendly.

Teddy might have been trying to be friendly, but he didn't succeed for long. The demon or whatever it was that lived inside of him suddenly woke up. "Let me try," he said, as he snatched the rod from Frisk's hand.

"Come on, Teddy. Give it back."

"After I'm finished," Teddy growled. "Maybe."

Frisk was more or less helpless. With spirits sinking he stood and watched as Teddy walked to the far end of the bridge and cast his new Mepps Silver Spinner into the river. Frisk's only real option was to wait and see what happened next.

He didn't have to wait long. Soon a large GMC flatbed truck appeared on the road to the bridge. It slowed as it approached the crossing, then came to a creaking halt beside Teddy. A man got out. It was Frank Wald, Teddy's father.

If Teddy was a bully, Frank was a tyrant. He addressed his son in a booming voice. "You were supposed to move that pile of pulp for me this afternoon."

Teddy cringed. "I know. I'm gonna."

"Darn right you're gonna," Frank barked. He turned an eye toward Frisk, who was watching the whole episode, then looked back at Teddy. "Where'd you get that fishing gear? Did you take it from that boy?"

"No," Teddy replied in a weak voice. "I borrowed it for a few minutes. He said it was okay."

Frank Wald glared at Teddy, then motioned for Frisk to come forward. As Frisk approached, Frank asked, "Did he take your rod?"

Frisk swallowed. "No sir. I told him he could try it out."

Frank huffed, shook his head in a dubious manner, then moved toward the idling truck. "Come on, Teddy. Give the boy his rod back. You've got a pile of pulp to move."

As Teddy extended the fishing rod, he hesitated long enough to establish eye contact with Frisk. Confusion and pain flooded Teddy's eyes, and for a second Frisk thought Teddy might cry. But of course he didn't cry. He lowered his gaze and hurried to the passenger door of the truck.

Frisk was filled with relief as the truck disappeared from view. He was thinking several thoughts at once: *That wasn't so bad. Sure glad Frank Wald isn't my father. No wonder Teddy is on edge all the time. Hmmm. Let's see, still a half an hour of light left. That wasn't too bad at all. No indeed.*

Chapter 10

In a word, *anxious* described the mood in the parlor on Friday. For the players, it was the last day of practice before the big show. For Frisk, well . . . he wasn't looking forward to seeing Teddy Wald. If he could've had his druthers, he would've gladly forgotten the encounter on the bridge. But he couldn't be sure of Teddy.

It was much to Frisk's relief that the day passed without Teddy showing his face in the Back Room.

Frisk was in bed with the lights out at nine-thirty on Friday night, yet sleep was not his companion. Although he was delighted that the tournament was finally to take place on the morrow, he was also a little sad. At the close of the day his role as the Back Room manager would end for the summer season.

Frisk was still awake at ten-thirty when Shelly dialed the telephone in the kitchen. He cocked an ear to listen. Including pauses that are not written, this was what he heard: "Hi Rachel. I hope I didn't wake you. Everything is fine. About an hour ago. He's got a big day tomorrow. Yes. So guess what, I think I found a place. Umhmm. That's why I called. Oh gosh, Rachel, it's the cutest little house in the world. Two bedrooms. One story. A huge yard. Marge took me this morning. Oh sure, she loved it. No, just one bath. Yes, a pantry with a washer and dryer. Forty-seven or forty-eight, I don't know yet. Definitely. Yep. I'm going early on Monday morning. No, not a clue. I'm sure he'll be surprised. Okay. Okay. Call me Monday night. Right. Bye, Rachel, I love you too."

Sleep continued to elude Frisk and his mind continued to churn. Although he was content to live in the apartment in town, he was immensely attracted to the idea of moving into a real house. He knew it would make Shelly happy, and he figured there would be plenty of room in the yard to keep a canoe.

Frisk was still trying to wrestle himself to sleep around midnight when his mind carried him back to the incident on the bridge with Teddy. Seeing the way that Frank Wald had treated his son gave Frisk a new understanding of Teddy. As he recalled the parting look Teddy had given him, it occurred to him that he'd seen a flicker of appreciation in Teddy's eyes. Frisk knew that he'd misread Teddy before, but even so, he now had the impression that Teddy had wanted to reach out and shake his hand . . . that Teddy had wanted to be friends.

A while later, Frisk drifted into dreamland.

The first thing Frisk did after he got dressed on Saturday morning was to sit down at his desk and make a sign that read No Tipping Today. The fifteen dollars the contestants had paid to enter the tournament covered all table fees, and Frisk thought it was only fair that the sum include gratuities. After all, the Wilma Eight Ball Tournament was the biggest event of the summer, and it was a privilege for him to be involved—he would rack the tables with pride. Not accepting tips would be his quiet way of saying thanks to the regular customers.

Billy Compton had instructed all entrants to be in the parlor a half hour before the games were slated to start at eleven. Frisk had everything ready by ten o'clock, and when he opened the door at ten-fifteen, Pepper greeted him with a wide grin. Once a year, on tournament day, the age restriction was lifted and youngsters like Pepper were allowed into the Back Room.

It was possible to fit just over forty people into the parlor. With twenty players having guaranteed entry, there was additional room for an audience of approximately twenty people. This space was taken on a first-come-first-serve basis.

Pepper stood with Frisk in the refreshment booth and watched as the parlor began to fill: Mr. Dean and Mr. Smittle shuffled in and took seats on the sofa. They were followed by Tim Reed and Winky Nelson, who leaned against the wall by the sofa. Art Blatt and Jason Farber entered and stood by Tim and Winky. Then came Vernon Beazely and Bingo Todd. They huddled around the Surf-rider pinball machine, and were soon joined by Ellard Castle, Clayton Burns, Rabbit Brooks, and Jimmy Simms.

Teddy Wald appeared at 10:26. As he was crossing the parlor to stand with Art and Jason, he nodded to Frisk and whispered, "Good morning, Frisk."

Frisk replied in kind, then shared an astonished look with Pepper. Teddy usually addressed Frisk as "Squirt," or "Wimp," but today he'd used Frisk's proper name. Coming from Teddy, that was no small sign of improved relations.

At 10:28 Dan Breedon entered the parlor carrying a steaming cup of coffee. He waved to Frisk, then crossed to sit on an arm of the sofa. He said hello to Mr. Dean and Mr. Smittle before taking a cautious sip from his cup.

As the Back Room continued to fill, Frisk began to worry about whether his mother would arrive in time to claim a spot. Finally, at 10:33, she slipped into the parlor and stood by the door. After winking at Frisk, she smiled at Dan, and then turned as Billy Compton strolled into the room. (His wife Delores was minding the store.) Billy carried a stool in one hand and a clipboard in the other. Every player present knew that the list of first-round matchups was attached to the clipboard.

Billy was the tournament director: He organized the event, kept the official records, judged disputes, and gave the final word on all that mattered. No one ever argued with Billy. He crossed the room and placed the stool in front of the locked red fire-door. A kind of expectant hush fell over the crowd as he sat down. Everyone was eager to learn who would be playing whom in the first round.

The tournament was organized as follows: Names were drawn from a hat to match players in the first round. With twenty players, there were ten matchups in the first round. To advance, a player had to win two out of three games. Winners advanced to the second round, where there were five matchups. Again, winners advanced to the third round. Then the rules changed and the five players in the third round played single-game matches. These matches were rotated so that each contestant faced a different opponent after each game. When a player lost two games, he was eliminated. Eventually, only two players would remain. These survivors then competed in a best-out-of-three series, with the winner becoming the tournament champion.

Although this might sound like a complicated system, it worked and was fair for all.

Billy had been seated for less than a minute when the president of the local bank, Blanton Ferris, entered the parlor. With him was his daughter, Beverly. She was fifteen. If an already hushed crowd could hush again, that was what happened now. Billy greeted the latecomers with a nod, then Blanton and his daughter sidled next to Shelly and tried to blend in with the crowd. They weren't very successful.

Beverly Ferris had big brown eyes and long, silky hair as red as the hair on Frisk's head. She was tall and slender and had curves in all the right places. She moved with the confident ease of an athlete. Today she wore blue jeans and a yellow blouse. Her hair was in a ponytail that fell to the small of her back.

Every player in the room stared at Beverly, yet it was not her good looks that had grabbed their attention; it was the custom-made cue stick she held at her side.

As the contestants began to digest the fact that a girl had entered the Wilma Eight Ball Tournament, the hush in the parlor gave way to mumbles and groans. Girls had been in the Back Room on previous occasions—sisters had come to fetch brothers, mothers had poked their heads in looking for sons, girlfriends had delivered messages to boyfriends—but no one present had ever seen a girl carry a cue stick into the parlor before. Surely none of the regulars had ever imagined such a sight.

Soon the mumbles turned to chuckles, and several of the guys started making funny faces. Mr. Dean and Mr. Smittle eyed the clownish offenders disapprovingly. Not only did the older gentlemen think it was rude to mock Beverly, they suspected that the mockers might soon be in for a shock. Both Mr. Dean and Mr. Smittle had been to Blanton Ferris's house and had seen the pool table in the basement. They also knew the Ferrises were modest and practical people, and it was likely that if Beverly had signed up for the tournament, it was because she had good reason to believe she could win.

Chapter 11

The chuckling and the face making ceased abruptly at five minutes to eleven when Billy stood to announce the pairings for the first round. In a flash, the mood in the parlor turned sharply serious. Like soldiers waiting for the battle to begin, the contestants communed with their own thoughts and grappled with jumpy nerves. The time to shut up and shoot well was at hand. There was one hundred dollars at stake for the winner. Now as friends looked across the room, instead of seeing friends, they saw opponents.

When Billy called out the matchups, he also assigned table numbers to the players and announced the order in which the matches would take place. "First game on table one, Art Blatt and Vernon Beazely. First game on table two, Dan Breedon and Rabbit Brooks. First game on table three, Teddy Wald and Winky Nelson. Second game on table one, Tim Reed and Jimmy Simms. Second game on table two, Beverly Ferris and

Mike White. Second game on table three, Jason Farber and John Chandler. Third game on table one, Scott Calhoun and Wally Moss. Third game . . ."

Frisk turned his gaze to Mike White and looked for signs of how Mike felt about facing Beverly in the first round. At a glance, Mike appeared calm and confident. His shoulders were relaxed and his arms were crossed in front of him. But Frisk was gazing, not glancing, and he was able to penetrate Mike's facade. His eyes gave him away. In them Frisk saw flickers of doubt. He supposed it was likely that Mike was afraid of going down in history as the first guy to lose to a girl in Compton's Billiard Parlor.

At 11:04 coins were flipped on all three tables, then the first round of the Wilma Eight Ball Tournament began. Frisk had racked the tables earlier that morning, so now there was nothing for him to do but watch and wait. He focused on the match between Dan and Rabbit. He wanted to see if there was any truth to the theory that Dan would've grown rusty after four weeks away from the parlor. Dan won the coin flip and chose to break. Shortly thereafter it was evident that the theory was hollow. Rabbit never had a chance. Six minutes later Frisk was racking the balls on table two. Dan executed an even break, and eight minutes later the match was over.

"Sorry," Dan said sincerely as he shook Rabbit's hand.

"That's all right." Rabbit smiled weakly. "I reckon the money is for a good cause."

Meanwhile, on table one, Art Blatt and Vernon Beazely were still chasing the eight ball in their first game. After an ugly sequence of missed shots, Art sank the eight. Another seventeen minutes would be needed for him to sink the eight again and win the match in two straight games.

Although some of the guys attempted to conceal the extent of their curiosity, they were all watching when Mike White flipped the coin for the second match on table two. Beverly Ferris called heads. Heads it was.

Frisk could see that Beverly had a slight case of nervous jitters as she stepped to the table and prepared to break. He also noted that she held her cue stick with good form. A low ball fell when she broke the rack, but she hurried her next shot and it rolled wide of the intended pocket. On Mike's turn he sank four high balls in a row before missing. Beverly approached the table, but the cue ball was in a bad position and she wasn't able to get a clear shot at any low balls. When she tried, she missed completely. Mike sighed with relief and returned to the table. When his turn was over the high balls were gone and the eight had disappeared into the side pocket.

The Back Room regulars commended Mike with sly winks and smug grins. It did not appear as if the girl in the yellow blouse was much of a threat. Frisk wasn't so quick to draw a conclusion. Beverly had only had one open shot and he was reserving judgment until she got another chance to prove herself.

Beverly's eyebrows were drawn downward and her chin jutted with determination as she waited for her turn in the second game. When it came, she stepped swiftly up to the table. This time the cue ball was in the open. She took aim and shot. *Clack*. She shot again. *Clack*. She paused and studied the table, then *clack*. Beverly was definitely more relaxed. She was on a roll.

Mike White bit his upper lip and stared straight ahead like a zombie. He'd just made history. It didn't feel very good.

Frisk caught Beverly's eye as he racked for the third game, and for a brief moment, the two redheads contemplated each other with open interest. Frisk didn't know if he was imagining things, but it seemed to him that Beverly was looking to him for reassurance. He felt as if he could read her thoughts: *I know I'm an outsider. Will you be my connection on the inside?* Frisk smiled, doing his best to make her feel welcome. He knew what it was like to be an outsider.

The third game between Beverly and Mike was

more evenly contested. It was decided when Beverly executed a beautiful bank shot on the twelve ball, then cut the eight into a side pocket. Mike White was out. He'd been eliminated by the girl.

Frisk took a quick look around the parlor. The only people grinning were Pepper, Blanton Ferris, Mr. Dean, and Mr. Smittle.

Chapter 12

The last game in the first round ended at a quarter after one, and Billy called for a half-hour break before the start of the second round. Several spectators, along with some of the contestants who had been eliminated, chose this moment to depart for home. Of those that stayed, a few frugal individuals opened lunch bags which they'd brought for the occasion. Mostly though, people rushed to the refreshment booth.

Frisk was besieged with orders. It seemed that everyone was speaking at once.

"Coke and a pack of Cheese Nabs."

"Orange juice and peanuts, please."

"Two Moon Pies."

"Potato chips and a root beer. Make it snappy, will ya?"

Frisk moved as fast as he could move, and eventually the crowd was more or less satisfied. After handing Pepper a Brown Cow he paused to catch his breath and look around the room. Dan was standing beside his mother, who was engaged in a conversation with Blanton Ferris. It wasn't much of a conversation. In fact, Blanton was listening while Shelly did all the talking. Frisk could see that she was excited about something.

Except for Bingo Todd, who relied on luck, the contestants playing in the second round of the tournament were better skilled than in the first round and subsequently the games went faster than before. The only match which lasted for more than half an hour was the duel between two best friends, Art Blatt and Jason Farber. In the end, Art cut his own throat when he scratched on the eight ball in the third game.

"Tough break," said Jason. He meant it too.

Art shrugged solemnly. "I guess if I had to lose, it might as well have been to you. Good luck."

"Thanks."

"You'll need it too. Did you notice how Beverly Ferris demolished Tim Reed in two straight games?"

Jason swallowed. "I saw a little. It looked worse than what she did to Mike in the first round."

The other second-round winners, along with Beverly and Jason, were Dan Breedon, Ellard Castle, and Teddy Wald. Miraculously, Teddy had survived the sloppy tactics of Bingo Todd.

Although several of the five contestants entering the third round were thinking they'd be happy as the runner-up, all were conscious of the hundred dollars that potentially belonged to them.

In the third round the competition shifted to single-game matches, to be played on table one and table two. First, Billy scribbled numbers on five pieces of paper, which he folded and put in a cap borrowed from Winky Nelson, then he instructed the remaining contestants to draw from the cap. The player selecting the highest number got to sit out the first game of the third round. Statistically, that player gained a small advantage. It just so happened that Dan Breedon drew the number five.

The player who lost the first game on table one was then paired against the player who had lost the first game on table two. The winners on table one and table two would be paired in alternating matches against the player who sat out the first game. Then the games would be rotated so the winner from each table played the loser from the other. Any contestant losing a total of two games was eliminated from the tournament.

Of the final five, Dan Breedon was the only one who appeared the least bit relaxed. The others wore expressions one might expect on a patient entering an operating room.

Teddy Wald drew the first game against Beverly

Ferris. He won the coin toss and chose to shoot first. He made the eleven ball on the break, then sank the ten and fifteen before relinquishing his turn. Beverly rattled the two ball in an end pocket, but it didn't fall. Teddy then proceeded to make the thirteen, fourteen, and twelve. When the eight ball fell where he called it he beamed with unrestrained pleasure.

Meanwhile, on table two, Jason Farber was in the act of defeating Ellard Castle. As Jason was taking aim at the eight ball, Teddy suddenly quit beaming. It had just dawned on him that his next opponent would be Dan Breedon.

Teddy did win the coin toss against Dan, but that was all he won. His only consolation (if you can call it that) was that Dan finished the game in short order.

In the game between the two players who lost their first game, Beverly quickly pulled ahead of Ellard Castle. *Clack,* the five ball fell. *Clack,* the three followed the five. *Clack. Clack.* The girl was on fire. *Clack,* the one ball disappeared. She pointed her nose, then *clack,* the eight ball dropped into a side pocket. Ellard had been eliminated from the tournament.

Ellard was hurting, yet he was gracious in defeat. "That was good shooting. For a girl, you really are pretty good."

"Should I take that as a compliment?"

Ellard blushed. "I meant, you're good and you are a girl."

"Thanks, Ellard. Thanks a lot."

Jason and Teddy played the next game on table one, while Beverly and Dan competed on the table beside them. Most of the attention in the room was directed toward table two. If Dan won it would constitute two losses for Beverly.

Dan executed a solid break, then proceeded to sink five object balls in a row. The audience couldn't help but be impressed with his masterful handling of a cue stick. Frisk looked proudly at Pepper and mouthed the words, "That's my teacher. He doesn't make mistakes." Pepper nodded that he understood, but then, after Dan's next shot, Pepper grimaced and looked away from Frisk. Dan made his shot, yet in doing so he sent the cue ball careening off the rail. It knocked the eight ball into an end pocket. The shock waves in the parlor were palpable. Without taking a single shot, Beverly Ferris had won the game.

Frisk caught Dan's eye and shrugged. Dan responded with a barely perceptible wink. He didn't seem upset. Indeed, there was something about the look in his eye that made Frisk wonder if Dan had intentionally lost the game. Was it possible? Had Dan knocked the eight ball in on purpose?

A moment later Jason triumphed over Teddy. Teddy made a show of being disappointed, but he wasn't terribly let down. The fact was, Teddy was pleased to have lasted into the final round.

With his win over Teddy, Jason became the only player left in the third round who had not lost a game. One could see from his expression that he knew this was both a good thing and a crummy thing. It meant that in the next two games he'd have to face Dan Breedon and Beverly Ferris.

The action was now limited to table one. As Frisk racked the balls on that table, Billy Compton looked up from his clipboard and said, "Dan, you got the draw to start the round, so you play first against Ellard. Beverly, you sit out for a game."

Jason won the coin flip. The balls scattered well on the break, but nothing fell for Jason. When Dan stepped forward to survey the lay of the table, it was apparent to everyone that the reigning champion was in a no-nonsense mood. *Clack*. Then *clack* again, and *clack*. Almost before Jason realized what had hit him, Dan had won the game.

As Frisk racked for the next game he felt Beverly's brown eyes resting on him, and he looked up to meet her gaze. The first time they'd made eye contact Frisk had gotten the feeling that she was trying to establish a connection in the parlor, but now he got a different impression. This time it seemed as if she was thinking: *If I can only win this game, I'll have a shot at the championship*.

It was a close game—very close. Near the end

Jason almost cut the eight ball into a side pocket. But unfortunately for him, almost wasn't good enough.

When Beverly sank the eight where it belonged, her father could restrain himself no longer. He thrust a fist in the air and cried, "Way to go, sweetheart!"

Blanton Ferris's outburst caused a ripple of polite laughter that lasted for several seconds. When it subsided the parlor grew eerily silent—the result of shock and chagrin. Jason was out. The Wilma Eight Ball Tournament had boiled down to Beverly Ferris and Dan Breedon.

The only people who didn't seem stunned by the situation were Mr. Dean and Mr. Smittle. Neither of them were blatant about it, but both of them had I-could've-told-you-so expressions on their faces.

Chapter 13

This was it, Frisk thought as he racked the balls on table one and looked around the parlor. Two more games, maybe three, and his stint as the Back Room manager was over for the year. He would apply again. Yet at this moment he was feeling sentimental. These people were his community. Although he wasn't really a member of the regular crowd, they were his friends.

And now, the final match. Frisk allowed that Beverly had some talent, but if gambling was allowed in the Back Room, he would've put his money on Dan. There was no doubt about it, Dan had the best touch.

After winning the coin toss, Dan squared his shoulders to the cue ball and drove his cue stick forward in a blur of controlled motion. *Whack!* The cue ball plowed into the waiting pile. The sound of the collision echoed throughout the parlor, restoring confidence to those regulars who had begun to fear an upset. It was an even break. Object balls scattered like so many colored marbles spilled on a slanted floor. In rapid succession the five, the ten, and the eleven ball dropped into various pockets.

Dan paused to study the table, and chalked the tip of his stick. As he bent forward and prepared to shoot, something no one could have anticipated happened—something startling and yet familiar to the residents of Wilma. The alarm at the fire house began to blare.

Eyebrows lifted. Jaws dropped open. The siren repeated its loud wail.

Some people in the parlor might have wondered what Dan Breedon would choose to do. But Dan didn't wonder. Before the siren could blare a third time, he propped his cue stick against the table and told Billy, "I gotta go."

"Sure. Of course," Billy said hurriedly, pointing a thumb to the emergency exit. "You parked out back? I'll open this door."

"My car is out front." Dan turned to leave.

Billy raised his voice as the siren sounded again. "Don't worry about the tournament. I'll postpone the final match until tomorrow."

Dan halted and spun on his heels. "No. Don't postpone it. I'd like to appoint a substitute to shoot for me."

"A substitute?"

"Yep." Dan turned to face the Back Room manager. "Frisk, will you fill in for me?"

Although Frisk could see that Dan was eager for a reply, he was temporarily too flabbergasted for words. Soon, though, he managed to reply in a squeaky voice, "I'll do my best."

Shelly was still standing next to Blanton Ferris by the door, and just before Dan passed through it he caught her eye and smiled. Then he was gone. He never saw the blushing, flustered look that appeared on Shelly's face. No one else saw the look either. At that moment all eyes in the Back Room had turned to Frisk.

Frisk could feel the sudden scrutiny as if it was a four-legged animal with horns. When he looked around, he didn't see faces, he saw question marks. No one present had ever seen him shoot at a pool ball before. They weren't even sure if he was tall enough to reach the table.

As the last echo of the fire siren died in the distance, the Back Room regulars began to moan and groan. As far as any of them could imagine, it was all over but the crying. A girl was going to win the tournament.

Beverly didn't exactly dance with joy, yet she did bounce from foot to foot and exude lots of cheery optimism.

Frisk felt a definite weight upon his shoulders. Dan had picked him—he'd been asked to fill in for the best player in town. And not only that, but he felt a sense of obligation to the Back Room regulars. They were the ones that had kept the parlor going all summer. Without them, there would have been no need for a manager. Forget the fact that Beverly was a girl. She was an outsider. She shouldn't be allowed to waltz in and walk away with the championship.

Frisk grabbed Dan's cue stick and stared steadily at Beverly. This time, there was nothing soft or empathetic about the exchange. Now it was redhead against redhead.

When Frisk spoke, his voice didn't squeak. "I believe it's my shot. Since Dan made two high balls and one low ball on the break, it's also my choice."

"That's right," Beverly agreed. She had stopped bouncing on her feet. Something about Frisk's cool manner had put a dent in her optimism.

Frisk took high balls. Two of them had already fallen and there was a relatively easy shot available on the thirteen. He made the shot, but any modest player might have done the same and it was too soon for the regulars to know if he was skilled or not. The next obvious shot for Frisk was on the twelve ball, but the cue ball was lying near the center of the table and he could not easily approach the shot. "Pardon me," he said to Beverly, then went to retrieve the wooden crate.

On his way into the refreshment booth Frisk brushed past Pepper, who now watched his friend with a mixture of awe, envy, and pride. After all, this was a pretty big moment in the town of Wilma, and Frisk was only twelve.

Mumbles of curiosity became sighs of understanding as Frisk placed the crate on the floor by table one and stepped onto his makeshift platform. But before he could shoot, Beverly turned to Billy in protest. "Mr. Compton. Isn't there a rule that says a player has to keep one foot on the floor at all times?"

Billy's face twitched ambiguously as he considered the question. Finally, he nodded. "Yes, keeping one foot on the floor is a house rule. But there's also a house rule that no one under the age of fifteen may shoot pool in the parlor. Since we're playing under unusual circumstances, I'm allowing the rules to be bent. Unless you object." Billy paused for a second, then added, "Of course we could wait and finish the match tomorrow with Dan."

Displaying a mature sense of humor, Beverly smiled knowingly at Billy and replied, "Actually, Mr. Compton, it's fine with me if Frisk uses the crate. I was just inquiring about the rules."

"Very well," said Billy. "Frisk, you may continue."

Frisk concentrated before he took his shot. *Clack*, the cue ball struck the twelve ball, and it rolled into a side pocket. With his left foot, and without taking his eyes from the table, Frisk slid the crate to a new position. He stepped up and squared his shoulders. *Clack.* The fourteen rolled into an end pocket. A moment later the nine did the same.

The guys in the room began to bubble with excitement. It was clear that Frisk knew what he was doing. A feeling of renewed hope surged through the parlor. At this moment, Frisk's status was elevated. He was no longer just a skinny kid who sold peanuts and racked the tables. Now he was defending the reputation of the Back Room regulars and he had become their brother. He was their peer. Only he could save them from major embarrassment.

Clack. The fifteen rattled in an end pocket and bounced out. Even so, the tide of hope did not abate.

As Frisk slid the crate away from the table he was thinking: *I could have made that shot. Concentration. That's the key to good shooting.*

At this moment Teddy Wald stepped forward and laid a chummy hand on Frisk's shoulder. "You're doing great," he whispered. "Just hang in there, man. We're rooting for you."

Frisk accepted Teddy's support with a nod and turned to watch Beverly. It was hard for him to fathom, yet here he was in the final round of the tournament . . . and there was Teddy Wald cheering him on.

Beverly now realized that Frisk Tilden was not

the pushover she had initially taken him for. She was already four balls behind in the game. If she was going to survive, she was going to have to shoot at the peak of her abilities. Paramount in her mind was the driving thought: *After coming this far, it sure would be a shame to lose to a kid.*

Clack. She sank the three ball. *Clack.* She sank the seven. *Clack.* The two fell, but then so did the cue ball. Beverly had scratched.

It was Frisk's shot at the fifteen, which was still sitting near the end pocket where it had rattled out.

Clack. The fifteen fell and the cue ball rolled into a perfect position for shooting at the eight. He didn't need the crate. *Clack.* When the game ball dropped from view the Back Room erupted in cheers. Frisk had won the first game.

Chapter 14

When Frisk moved to rack the table for the next game, Billy slid off his stool and waved him aside. "I'll do that. You're a contestant now."

"Yes sir," Frisk said softly. It seemed stranger than strange that Billy would rack for him.

Frisk glanced at Shelly and saw that the first two fingers on her right hand were crossed. Beside her stood Blanton Ferris. He didn't have his fingers crossed, but it did look like he was mumbling some sort of prayer.

Frisk spread the balls evenly when he broke, yet not one of them fell into any pocket. Beverly took full advantage of the open table. When she was done the upbeat mood in the Back Room had been seriously tempered. Frisk got another chance, but it wasn't much of one. With the cue ball hidden on the rail behind the eight, his only option was a wild shot—or, as the regulars called it, a Bingo Todd.

Frisk's wild shot resulted in Beverly having a

straight-in on the eight ball. She stepped swiftly to the table and aimed. *Clack.* Now they were tied at one game apiece.

It suddenly got so quiet in the parlor that everyone could hear Winky Nelson scratching his head. Beverly's win had been impressive. The tide of support was still with Frisk, yet a dark shadow had been cast in the minds of the regular crowd.

While Billy racked for the third and deciding game, Frisk studied the floor. The burden of the moment was tremendous. A part of him wished he was sitting on a shady bank of the Turkey Scratch, instead of standing in the spotlight in Compton's Billiard Parlor. But that was just a part of him, and he looked up when he heard pool balls clacking on the break. He'd told Dan he would do his best. He could sit by the river any day.

Beverly sank one object ball after the break, then hurried her next shot and missed the pocket by two inches. Evidently, Frisk wasn't the only contestant feeling the pressure.

Now concentrate, he reminded himself as he stepped onto his crate and prepared to shoot the eleven ball. *Clack.* The eleven hesitated on the lip of the pocket . . . then dropped. He moved the crate. *Clack,* the nine ball dropped. Then the twelve. It was followed by the fourteen. As he shot at the ten ball he silently cautioned himself: *I'm not concentrating. I'm going too fast.*

Sure enough, the ten veered wide of the intended pocket.

When Beverly returned to the table she had regained her composure, and as if to drive home the point, she made five shots in a row before relinquishing her turn. For Frisk, the situation looked dour. Only one of Beverly's object balls remained on the table.

Frisk had three balls to go before the eight, and the way things stood he was pretty sure he would have to make them all to win the game. Win the game, he thought. What a strange concept. If he won the game he won the match. And if he won the match . . . well, he would win the championship.

Concentrate. That's the key to good shooting.

Clack. The ten ball disappeared from the table. He was still alive. Slowly, carefully . . . then *clack,* the thirteen was gone.

Now they were dead even. Beverly began to shift her weight from foot to foot. She wasn't dancing; it was a nervous reaction.

You could have heard a mouse sneeze as Frisk squared his shoulders and prepared to shoot the fifteen. Then the door to the parlor swung open and broke his concentration. It was Dan Breedon. Dan was sweating and he had soot on his hands and face, but he was okay.

With everyone staring at Dan, he felt compelled

to account for his actions. "It was a brush fire behind Milton Green's garage. We put it out before it could spread to the house."

"Good work," said Billy. The sentiment was echoed by a dozen others.

Dan turned to where Frisk was poised over the table. The sight caused the handsome firefighter to chuckle. "I'll be darned. I see you're still kicking."

"I guess I am," Frisk answered with a quick grin.

"They're tied at one game apiece," called Ellard Castle.

"Dead even," added Jason Farber.

With a great sigh of relief Frisk stepped off his crate and held the cue stick out to Dan. "I'm sure glad you're back. You can take it from here."

"Oh no." Dan laughed and took a step backward. The move just happened to place him next to Shelly Tilden. "I got the fire. You finish the game."

Chapter 15

Frisk took aim at the remaining object ball and did his best to block out the crowd. He, along with everyone else, held his breath as he thrust his cue stick forward. It felt like he was in a dream when the fifteen ball rolled into a side pocket.

His own voice seemed alien to him when he announced, "Eight ball in the end."

Clack. In the next instant Frisk heard Pepper scream, "You got 'em, Frisk. You did it!"

Then he felt himself rising into the air. Art Blatt and Jason Farber had hoisted him onto their shoulders.

"Incredible! And I didn't even know you could shoot."

"Right on, Mister Frisk!"

"He's the man."

A moment later Frisk was lowered to his feet. Immediately a throng of well-wishers surrounded him. Everyone insisted on shaking his hand and congratulating him personally. Of all the accolades he received, none were more appreciated than the words of Teddy Wald. "Good going, Frisk. I'm sorry I acted like a jerk this summer. I guess I wasn't thinking right."

"That's okay, Teddy," Frisk said sincerely. "No harm done."

"I didn't mean any either." Teddy gave Frisk a firm yet friendly slap on the back. "Maybe we can go fishing together sometime this fall."

"Maybe." Frisk nodded, then stepped out of the circle of Back Room regulars and walked over to Beverly Ferris.

She greeted him with a smile. "Congratulations. You're pretty good with a stick."

"So are you," Frisk said respectfully.

As the two redheads were shaking hands Billy approached and presented the runner-up with a fifty-dollar bill. "This is for you, Beverly. You impressed a lot of people today."

"Thank you, Mr. Compton."

"I'm glad you did well in your first tournament."

"So am I," Beverly said cheerfully.

Billy smiled, then turned to Frisk and extended two fifty-dollar bills.

Frisk held up a hand in protest. "Oh no. That belongs to Dan. I was just substituting."

Dan and Shelly walked over to where Billy and

Frisk were standing. "Take it, Frisk," said Dan. "You earned it."

"Not really," said Frisk. "You got me to the final round. And I didn't pay an entry fee. It's yours, Dan. You take it."

Dan chuckled. "No, Frisk, it's yours."

Frisk paused before replying, "I tell you what. If you let me pay half the entry fee, we can split the prize money."

Now it was Dan's turn to pause. Finally, he agreed. "Okay, we can split the money, but only if you let me take you and Shelly to a good restaurant in Richmond."

Frisk smiled. That sounded fine with him. "Mom. Is that all right with you?"

Although the expression on Shelly's face said yes, she answered aloud anyway. "That's more than all right with me."

That very evening Frisk and Shelly got into Dan's Impala and headed to Richmond. Frisk sat in the backseat with the window down. It was a satisfying ending to a remarkable day. They hadn't traveled far when Shelly shared her secret about buying a house on the outskirts of Wilma. Now that Blanton Ferris had said she would probably qualify for a loan, she was much too excited to hide her dream any longer.

Dan, who had overheard her speaking with

Blanton, said it was a good thing to own a house. He had been thinking about buying one too.

Without thinking too deeply about what he was doing, Frisk chose this moment to tell his mother about his savings account. "With my share of the prize money and the paycheck Billy gave me, after I make my deposit on Monday, I'll have over two hundred dollars in the bank. Mom, I'd like to lend it to you to help pay for the house."

"Frisk—" Shelly's voice cracked with emotion. "That's very generous of you. Very generous. But I can't take your money."

"Why, Mom?" Frisk leaned forward. "Why won't you take the money? You're going to let me live in the house, aren't you?"

Shelly turned to the backseat. "Yes, Frisk, I'm going to let you live there. But I've been saving for this for a long time, and . . . well, it wouldn't be appropriate for me to borrow money from you. Thank you just the same. I'm proud of you for offering."

After Shelly turned her head to face forward again, Frisk asked one last time, "Are you sure?"

Shelly laughed happily. "Frisk, if the money is burning a hole in your pocket, you might buy a bicycle so you can ride back and forth to town."

"Okay." Frisk thought that was a splendid idea. "And Mom, while I'm out buying stuff, maybe I'll get a canoe to put the bike under when it rains."

Dan laughed along with Shelly.

Frisk leaned back in the seat and stuck his right arm out the window. It felt good the way the wind moved his hand up and down. In fact, he was feeling good all over—as good as he could remember ever feeling. Already in his mind, he knew the time had passed when anyone from Wilma would bother to feel sorry for him or Shelly again.

The seven balls below the eight are called low balls; the others are called high balls. In eight ball, one player shoots at low balls and the opposing player shoots at high balls. The balls can be shot in any order. After players have put all the balls in their group (low or high) into any of the pockets on the table, they then shoot at the eight ball. The winner is the player who sinks the eight without scratching. A player scratches when the cue ball falls into a pocket. It is possible to scratch whether you sink an object ball or not.

A cue stick is used to strike the cue ball and propel it toward an object ball. Cue sticks are taller than the average teenager. They are smooth and tapered to a firm, circular tip at one end. The tip is used to strike the cue ball.

There are many additional facts associated with eight ball. There are terms for holding the cue stick, terms for putting spin on the cue ball, terms for strategies, and terms for different shots—yet knowing the terms is no substitute for actually playing the game. It is immensely popular for one simple reason: It's fun.

Lots of fun. You might give it a try sometime.

About Eight Ball

For those readers who have never played eight ball, here are a few basic facts about the game.

Eight ball is played on a rectangular table that has six pockets for receiving pool balls. A regulation table is nine feet by four and a half feet. It stands thirty and a half inches tall. The surface is made of slate covered with tightly stretched felt, usually green.

The interior sides of the table are called rails. The rails are cushioned so that a moving ball will ricochet, or bounce away upon impact. When a player intentionally bounces a ball off a rail, it is called a bank shot.

Sixteen balls are used to play eight ball. One of them is all white. This is the cue ball. It is used to knock the other balls, called object balls, into the six pockets. Object balls are numbered one through fifteen. Balls one through eight are solid colored. Balls nine through fifteen have white stripes over colors. The eight is the only black ball on the table.

Other Books by Hysteria Publications

College: The Best Five Years of Your Life by Clark Benson and Alex Gordon (paperback, $12.95)

Getting in Touch with Your Inner Bitch by Elizabeth Hilts (paperback, $7.95)

The Noisy Passage: Baby Boomers Do Menopause by Marie Evans and Ann Shakeshaft (paperback, $8.95)

Dates for the Greats: A Personal Ads Parody from Adam & Eve to Sigmund Freud by Doris Chelmow and Harold Rand (paperback, $8.95)

Pandemonium: Or, Life with Kids, a collection of parental humor (paperback, $8.95)

'Cause I'm the Mommy (That's Why!) by Donna Black (paperback, $7.95)

A Useless Guide to WindBlows95 by Murkysoft (paperback, $7.95)

Power Parenting Your Teenager

Power Parenting Your Teenager

Mary Eve Corbel

Bridgeport, Connecticut

First United States edition

ISBN 1-887166-14-9

Printed in the United States

For more information, contact:

PO Box 8581
Bridgeport, CT 06605
Tel: 203.333.9399
Fax: 203.367.7188
E-mail: hysteria@bridgeport.com
Web: http://www.bridgeport.com/hysteria

Distributed to the trade by Andrews and McMeel
Order department and customer service toll-free number: 800.826.4216
Order only fax: 800.437.8683

First published by Arsenal Pulp Press, Vancouver, 1991
with the title *Don't Say No, Just Let Go*

Cover cartoon by Nicole Hollander
Cover and interior design by David Charlsen
Typesetting by Jeff Brandenburg, ImageComp

Contents

PREFACE
Welcome to Power Parenting! viii

PART ONE
Toxic Teens, Poisoned Parents

CHAPTER 1
The Toxic Teen 3

CHAPTER 2
The Five Parts of a Teen 7

CHAPTER 3
Co-Teening No More! 12

CHAPTER 4
A Professional Dialogue 18

PART TWO
Empowering the Power Parent

CHAPTER 5
Learning to Let Go 23

CHAPTER 6
Parent Throttling 29

CHAPTER 7
Teensactional Analysis 35

CHAPTER 8
Communicating with Teens 40

CHAPTER 9
Teen Health 50

CHAPTER 10
Timeless Paths of Power Parenting 53

CHAPTER 11
Letting Go, Kicking Out & Living It Up 61

CHAPTER 12
The One-Minute Mother 64

PART THREE
Getting from Where You Are to Where You Wanted to Be in the First Place

CHAPTER 13
The Power Parenting Check-In 71

CHAPTER 14
The Power Parenting Bookshelf 75

CHAPTER 15
Power Parenting Enhancement Products 78

INDEX 81

List of Figures

Comparative Stress Levels of Some Life Events x
Physical Effects of Teen Toxicity 5
The Five Parts of a Teen 7
The Parts of a Teen (Age 14) 9
The Parts of a Teen (Age 18) 10
A Typical Co-Teening Genogram 15
The Seminar Table 19
Power Parenting Through the Ages 38
The Parent Mind-Map 41
The Teen Mind-Map 42
Teen Curfew Egg Chart 48
Teen–Parent Biorhythm Intersection Chart 52
Pendulum Power 55
The Parent's Brain 56
Chaos Power 59

ACKNOWLEDGMENTS

Power Parenting Your Teenager was conceived and written with the help of Jo Cook, Sandra Currie, Stephen Osborne, Peg Thompson and Saeko Usukawa. By compulsively telling each other the truth, we managed to raise eleven teenagers and we lived to tell about it. So did they, and so will you.

—MEC

PREFACE

Welcome to Power Parenting!

This book grew out of a series of revelations that began when my children became teenagers, and I found myself thinking I must have died and gone to hell. Only yesterday, it seemed, I was lying in the hospital in my pink bed-jacket, cuddling a sweet little newborn and promising never to do all the terrible things to it that had been done to other children, including myself. But now, here I was, running through the house after a sullen, monosyllabic, existentialism-sodden monster. I was waving a pair of scissors in the air and screaming, "Well, then, I'll cut it for you!"

I knew then that I needed help.

Like many parents, I turned to the experts. (*Fact:* there are now 3.7 parenting experts per North American teenager.) I read their books, I went to their overpriced seminars, I cried in their offices. Worst of all, I tried to believe them when they described life with teens as a "challenge." My own experience told me that living with teens is not a "challenge"; living with teens is at best a bad dream and at worst a nightmare.

It began to dawn on me that my teens and I suffered most when I tried to follow the experts' advice to *do the right thing*, and—in one way or another—*deal with* my teenagers. On the other hand, I noticed that whenever I found myself *not* dealing with my teens, a pleasant, peaceful atmosphere prevailed briefly in our home. I felt strong, confident, in charge of my life and my household.

So I asked myself, how can I consistently *not deal with* my teens? Well, the solution was right in front of me, in my adult relationships. I don't know about you, but I have plenty of grown friends and relatives who make perfectly ludicrous life decisions. When they announce these decisions, I don't say, "No." I don't say, "Over my dead body." I say, "Great, good idea, let me know how it turns out." What if I applied this supportive nonconfrontation to my life with my adolescent children?

At first, not dealing with my teens proved to be much harder than I had thought it would be. I had to force myself not to rise to the bait that was constantly dangled in front of me.

Teen #1: I flunked out of school and I'm not going back.

Me (through tears and clenched teeth): OK.

Gradually, my effort of will paid off. I was developing a benign, Zen-like nondecision to deal with them.

Teen #2: School sucks, man. I'm out of there.

Me: Hmm.

Eventually, I began to experience a distinct lack of interest in dealing with them.

Teen #3: School is a capitalist plot. I'm quitting.

Me: Great, good idea, let me know how it turns out.

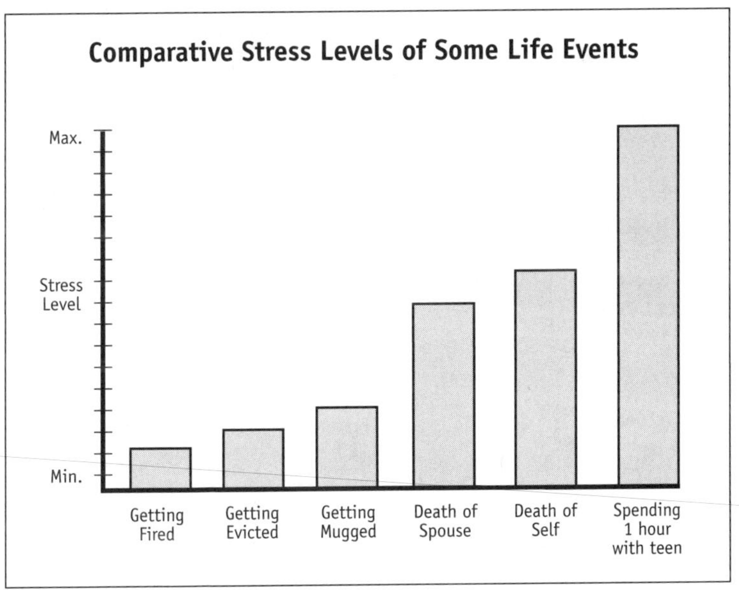

How liberating it was! My teens' new lifestyle enabled them to go ahead and do all the dumb stuff they were going to do anyway, and my new lifestyle enabled me to let go of my masochistic preoccupation with my teens and start writing down how I succeeded in not dealing with them.

Now I give these techniques to you—all the many creative ways of not dealing with teenagers that my friends and I have developed over the years. Together they are called the Power Parenting method, and their central philosophy is that there is only one way to get absolute power in your life with teens—Don't say no, just let go.

PART ONE

Toxic Teens, Poisoned Parents

CHAPTER

1

The Toxic Teen

You can spend years striving to understand teenagers and the syndromes of teenage life. Sure, teens are easy to pity, surrounded as they are by Clearasil, boom boxes, political causes and gang warfare. But take another look.

All around you, there are people in even deeper pain than teens: people who have yellow bags under their eyes, who cry themselves to sleep at night, whose hearts are swathed in scar tissue. No matter how much you study teens, these other people never go away. They are the victims of a devastating epidemic. They are the Poisoned Parents of Toxic Teens, and you may be one of them.

Do You Suffer from Teen Toxicity?

Well, you're reading this book, aren't you? And there are hundreds of other physical and psychic symptoms, including but not limited to the yellow bags mentioned above.

If any of the following scenarios is familiar to you, you may well be the victim of a Toxic Teen:

- Your 13-year-old daughter told you she was staying at a friend's house overnight, and her friend told her mother she was staying at your

place. Later you found out the two girls had been walking around downtown all night in their pink spandex short-shorts.

- You had your first date since you split up with your husband 7 years ago, and when you invited the date over for dinner, your son, 16, brought out all the old pictures of you and your husband in happier times.
- Your 17-year-old daughter took her entire share of a large family inheritance and bought a discarded, rusted-out, inoperative school bus with no windows or tires—from a "guy named Rick."
- When he goes out in public with you, your son wears a ski mask so that none of his friends will recognize him.

There is another dead giveaway: your sick tendency to cover up the emotional battering your teen has inflicted on you.

Example:

Your 16-year-old son and his friends were caught driving through funeral ceremonies and mooning the mourners. You went on a two-week crying jag and finally sought help, saying it was something you ate.

Example:

Your daughter, 14, was missing for two days, then phoned you to report that she had "caught a ride to Mexico" and needed you to wire her $200. By this time you had developed asthma, hives, rickets and hair loss. Incredibly, you told your doctor that your job was causing you a lot of stress.

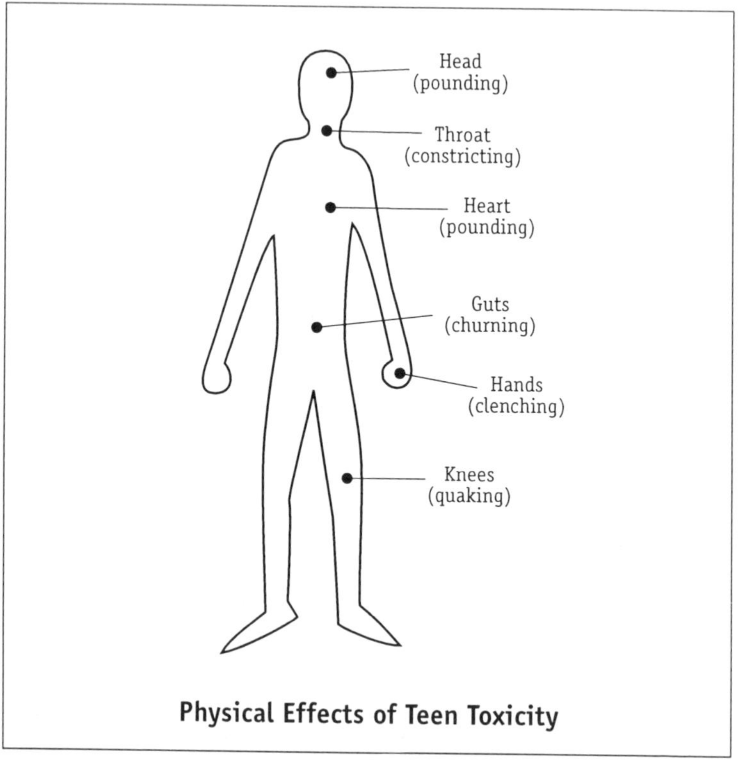

Physical Effects of Teen Toxicity

And remember—the problem crosses all economic and ethnic lines. While the details vary from family to family, all Toxic Teens leave the same scars (the yellow bags, for example).

What Causes Teen Toxicity?

There are experts who believe Toxic Teens are the product of over-permissive or over-repressive parents (parent-blaming is always in vogue with psycho-gurus, who have cushier jobs than parents). They will tell you that today's Toxic Teens are just yesterday's Toxic Tots—spitting puréed beet on freshly painted walls, secretly eating soap, unfurling rolls of toilet

paper, etc. Another school holds that Teen Toxicity is probably *hormonal*, and therefore timeless. We've all seen those ancient cave-paintings in which adolescents turn up their noses at homemade clothing or enjoy a clandestine smoke behind a grove of pre-petrified trees.

Well, let the experts believe what they want to believe. All the theories in the world are no use to the Poisoned Parent.

Can You Be Detoxified?

The condition is rarely fatal, but it is debilitating. The nervous disorders will probably disappear when your teens leave home (see Chapter 11), but other effects, such as the yellow bags, may be permanent.

You live with teens, so you have already figured out that you can't change a Toxic Teen. *But you can change yourself.* You can become a Power Parent.

Early Warning Signs of Teen Toxicity

Four Early Signs of Teen Toxicity (Verbal):

- "Everyone but me has a car."
- "I don't believe in birth control."
- "I can quit any time I want."
- "You can trust me."

Four Early Signs of Teen Toxicity (Behavioral):

- Maintaining absolute silence for more than 90 days.
- Eating more than 3 lbs. or less than 3 oz. of food at any one meal.
- Sleeping with car parts.
- Being brought home by police officers.

CHAPTER

2

The Five Parts of a Teen

The key to understanding your teen's bizarre behavior—toxic one minute, fun and friendly the next minute—is to recognize that every adolescent has five separate yet interrelated parts.

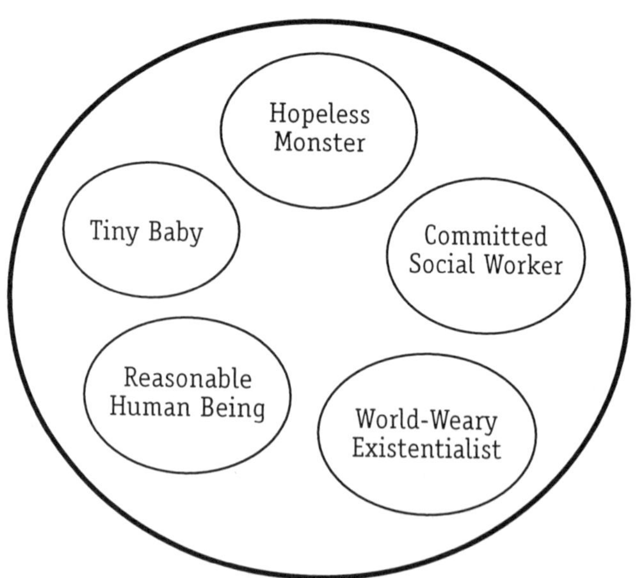

The Five Parts of a Teen

Emergence Differential of the Five Parts

Any of the five parts of your teen may surface at any given moment.

Example:

Wilf has just turned 16. His room is such a pigsty he can hardly shut the door.

Tiny Baby: Wilf refuses to clean his room, preferring to wallow in his own detritus as he did in the womb.

Committed Social Worker: Wilf chides you for being hung up on one messy room when millions of children are hungry.

World-Weary Existentialist: Wilf sighs, stares out at the rain and says that nothing matters, least of all the garbage festering in his room.

Hopeless Monster: Wilf screams, slams doors, hurls profane accusations and throws things when asked to return the eight coffee cups rotting in his room.

Reasonable Human Being: Wilf cleans up his room because he can't find his favorite leather bracelet with the chromed iron studs.

Example:

Renee, 15, has been invited to a huge mid-winter party, the social event of the tenth-grade.

Tiny Baby: Renee argues strongly to stay out late at the party, and begs you with all of her body language to stop her from going.

Committed Social Worker: Renee stays late at the party so she can organize her friends to attend the Anti-Everything rally next Friday.

World-Weary Existentialist: Renee goes to the party early and stays late, then comes home and pronounces it "dead boring, as usual."

Hopeless Monster: Renee screams, slams doors, hurls profane abuse and throws things because she has "nothing to wear" to the party.

Reasonable Human Being: Renee stays home from the party because she has to get up early for work, and anyway "Skeeter" is out of town that weekend.

Shifting Proportions of the Five Parts

At various stages in a teen's development, each of the five parts grows or shrinks in size. At age 14, the proportions look something like this:

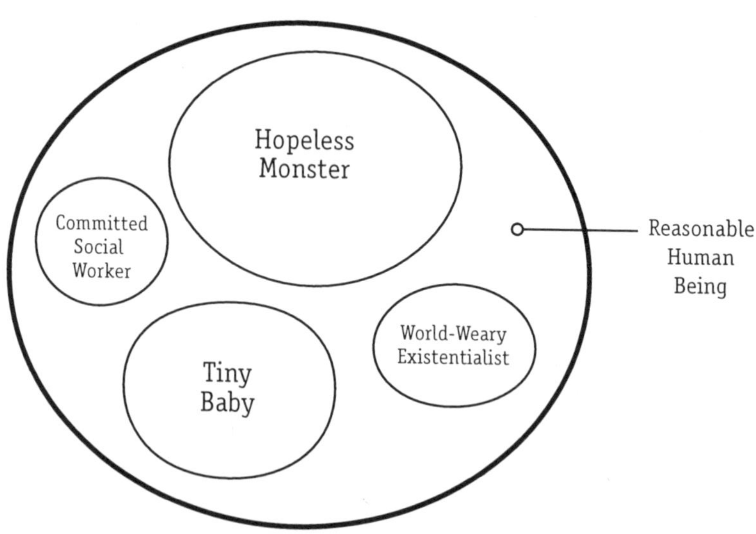

The Parts of a Teen (Age 14)

By age 18, you should expect a considerable change:

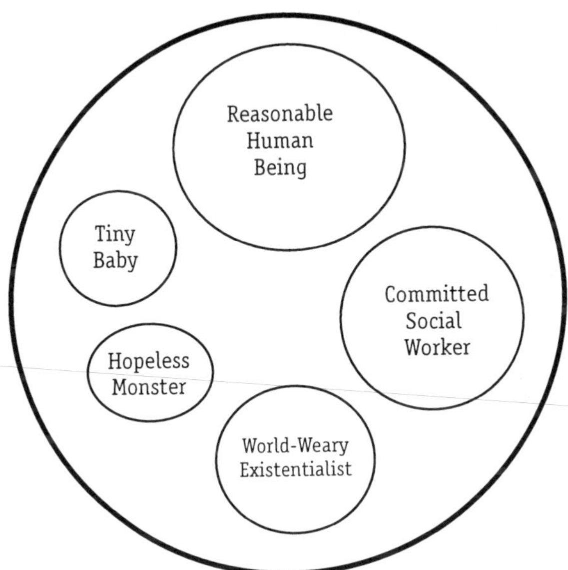

The Parts of a Teen (Age 18)

Not every teen develops in the same way or at the same rate. It is normal for the components to change size randomly—every year, every day, every minute.

Accepting the Five Parts: The Whole Teen Approach

Recognizing and identifying the five parts of your teen is the first step to Power Parenting. The second step is to ignore all of the five parts equally. This is known, in modern parlance, as the Whole Teen Approach.

More important, the true Power Parent takes the Whole Parent Approach to herself. She does not have five parts. She has one part: the part that wants to live free of teen-induced anxiety and guilt.

From Mary Eve's Mailbag

Dear Mary Eve:

My 18-year-old daughter has begun to advise me on make-up (I don't wear it) and fashion (I couldn't care less). She says, "Mom, you need Jojoba oil for those deep wrinkles around your eyes," and "This $20 peppermint foot oil should get the swelling down. I guess we can't do anything about the ankles." She has also plucked off all her eyebrows. Is she in the teen Committed Social Worker mode or is this really some kind of twisted Tiny Baby/Hopeless Monster revenge thing?

—*Confused* in Kansas City

Dear Confused:

Why bother to figure it out, when you could be tending your roses or writing letters to the President, or whatever it is you like to do? Get a life.

—*Mary Eve*

Dear Mary Eve:

My wife and I separated last year and agreed on shared custody. Now our two teens play us off against each other. When they come to my apartment, they say, "At Mom's we don't have a curfew," and when they go there, they say, "At Dad's, we can drink as much beer as we want." I respect very much the work you've done around single parenting and double parenting, but what about that gray area in between, separated parenting?

—*Struggling* in Seattle

Dear Struggling:

I recommend twist ties.

—*Mary Eve*

CHAPTER

3

Co-Teening No More!

What Is Co-Teening?

Co-teening is thinking, saying or doing anything that supports or encourages Toxic Teen behavior. You are probably thinking to yourself, "No way would I do a fool thing like that!" But no parent co-teens on purpose. Indeed, most of them *don't even know they are doing it!*

Characteristics of a Co-Teen

- Desperately wants her teen to do normal things, such as speaking without mumbling and developing a taste for books that have words in them.
- Cannot stop herself from teen-referencing: her reality check is never herself, but the unconscionable thing her teen did yesterday, is doing right now or is certain to do tomorrow.
- Experiences constant doubt, fear and panic.
- Believes her teens' outrageous behavior is somehow her own fault and wishes she had been a

better parent, though she wonders how this would have been possible.

The bad news is that if you have any of these tendencies, you are probably a co-teen. The good news is that co-teening, like many other unforgivable acts, has now been identified as a sickness. Which means that you are no longer alone! And you can be healed.

From Mary Eve's Mailbag

Dear Mary Eve:

I understand parents must get in touch with the Toxic Teen Within, but I think my wife is overdoing it. She bought us all 3-D glasses so we could watch a rock concert on cable TV, cooked macaroni and cheese for supper every night last week, and used my car without permission. Our room is a complete mess and she hasn't had a haircut in months! When I confronted her, she said, "So?" and "Why are you always picking on me?" What should I do?

—*Anxious* in Atlanta

Dear Anxious:

You have not yet grasped the essence of Power Parenting. Let go, even if it's your own wife. OK, she's gone overboard with the Teen Within stuff, but hey, she's feeling no pain. You, on the other hand, probably have eczema and palpitations. Relax, Anxious!

—*Mary Eve*

The Co-Teening Disease Process

There are four levels of co-teening behavior, ranging from the very subtle to the incredibly silly.

Level I Co-Teening: Bearing the Cross

Example:

Jillian, 13, has befriended a group of 17-year-old dropouts at the cappuccino bar. Father mopes around her, sighing heavily and looking burdened. She stays out later and later. Father goes gray and wrinkled. The school principal reports much cutting of classes. Father weeps silently into large snifters of brandy.

Level II Co-Teening: Trying to Fix It

Example:

The Thompson teens refuse to do any household chores. Mother and Father have become the Behavior Mod Squad, offering the teens extra allowance to do the chores, withholding all allowance when they do not do the chores, offering gourmet dinners when they do the chores, withholding all dinners when they do not do the chores, offering late model sports cars when they do the chores, etc.

Level III Co-Teening: Covering up

Example:

Chantelle has recently turned 14. When she smokes cigars in front of Father's business associates, he tells them she is

A Typical Co-Teening Genogram

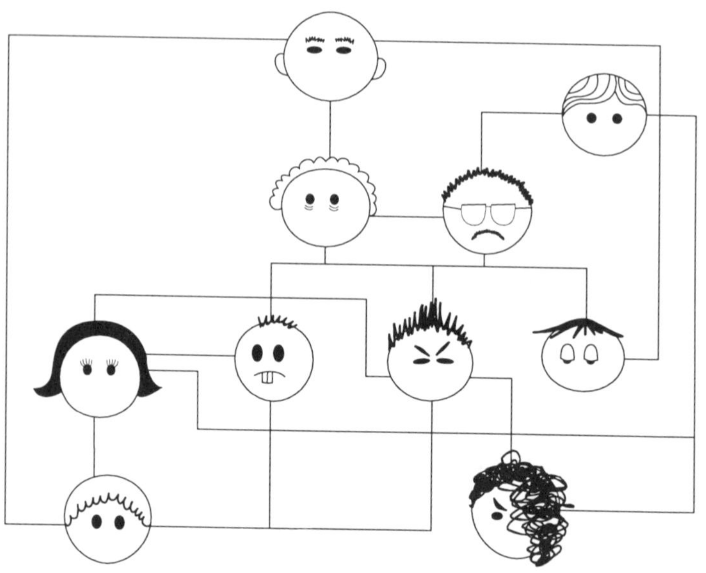

Mother of Teen

Toxic teen

Father of Teen

Toxic teen's best friend, also son of father's boss

Dormant toxic teen

Young child

Young child's good pal, who emulates toxic teen

Mother of good pal, whom young child likes better than real mother and whom toxic teen once saw nude

Father's boss,once married to cousin of young child's good pal's mother

Maternal grandfather of toxic teen, who loves dormant toxic teen best and suspects young child's good pal is his son

rehearsing for a school play. When she gets her head shaved and shows up during Father's party, he tells his friends she is having chemotherapy. When she engages his bridge club in conversation filled with s— and f—, he tells them she is a tragic victim of Tourette's Syndrome.

Level IV Co-Teening: Out-Teening the Teen

Example:

Bruce, 16, has fallen in with a motorcycle gang. Before long, Mother finds herself wearing skin-tight black leather garments, flipping the high sign to filthy men on Harley Davidsons and craving Jack Daniels for breakfast.

In all of these cases, the parent's life centers on the Toxic Teen. Therefore teens have no choice but to remain toxic, or what purpose in life do their parents have?

The Co-Teening Healing Process

Confronting the Toxic Teen Within

You were once a teen yourself, and you went to astonishing lengths to torment your parents. Remember? Get in touch with the Toxic Teen who still lurks in your psyche. Then you can take that first important step to joyful recovery.

Letting the Teen Within Do Without

Everyone has a Toxic Teen inside, but only the Power Parent gives that teen its voice, then ignores everything it says. Don't say no, just let go.

Healing the Battered Parent Within

Let's go back to our examples and offer those besieged families some Power Parenting solutions:

- Jillian's father has got to get a lover, or at least a personal computer.
- Mother and Father Tremblay should take up oil painting or lawn mower racing; then everyone in the family can relax.
- Why does Father keep inviting people over?
- As for Bruce's mother, let her experience remind us that there is a world of difference between "don't say no" and "me too."

CHAPTER

4

A Professional Dialogue

Recently I attended an international symposium on parenting teens. One controversial panel discussion was on Duplex Families: the Effect on Unrelated Teens of Their Single Parents Moving in Together. On the panel were some highfalutin professionals, Drs. Chan, Diego, Geist and Sidhu, and one token actual parent of teens—me. So that you might understand what Power Parents are up against at the "expert" level, here is an excerpt of that session.

Diego: I must posit that the transformational boundaries of the Duplex Family have serious phenomenological repercussions.

Chan: But within the interstices of a societal expectation, which still has a socio-evolutionary memory of the extended family, the resolution is not a true paradigm shift.

Corbel: Either way, they're going to be a pain in the neck until they're at least 19 years old.

Geist: There is an implication of a comprehension of the formation of adolescent psycho-intellectual evolution that transcends the relational confines of—

Sidhu: No, no! Forgive me for interrupting, Doctor, but there has been no instigation of a transposition

of the Duplex Causality Curve, crucial to any discussion of subjugation or liberation.

Corbel: Is anyone doing research on freeze-drying teens and thawing them out later, after we figure out what to do?

Diego: Interrelational stress tendencies may be interdeterminantly comparable, in the hegemony of the relational sphere.

Corbel: Yes, teenagers all over the world are impossible to live with.

Geist: Let me sum up, learned colleagues, with the proposition that the situational parameters of the Duplex Family impact substantially on dialogic signals in the parental inflow-outflow diametric.

Corbel: In other words, don't say no, just let go.

Sidhu: Hear! Hear!

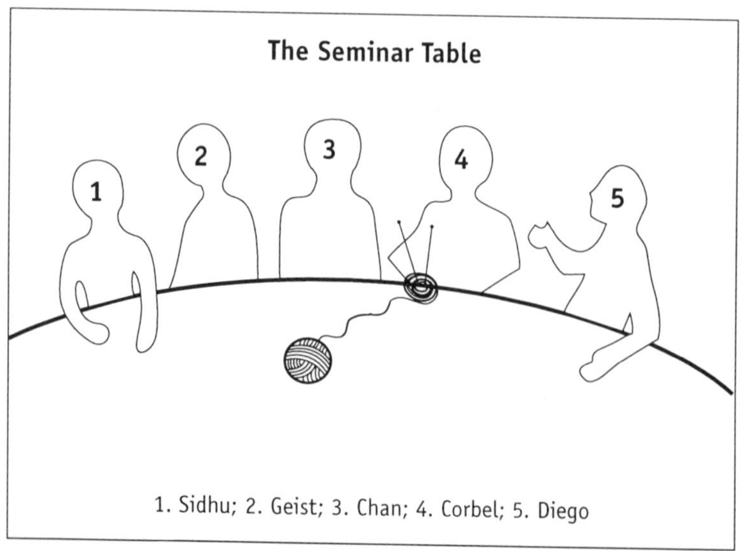

From Mary Eve's Mailbag

Dear Mary Eve:

Every time I come home from the grocery store, my twin teenaged daughters make a terrible fuss about the plastic bags, the laundry detergent and the bleached toilet paper. They refuse to eat any cookies made by companies that operate factories in the Third World. They stomp on American products to protest Free Trade. I would appreciate your advice.

—*Victimized* in Vancouver

Dear Victimized:

Rarely do I advise embryonic Power Parents to out-teen their teens, but in this case I must make the exception that proves the rule. You must begin shopping only at politically correct health food stores and co-ops. Within 14 days your teens will be so sick of sawdust breakfast cereal, fruit juice made by local but incompetent manufacturers, and unhomogenized milk swarming with gelatinous fat globules—all brought home in those cloth carry-bags that mush everything together and smell bad—that they will beg you to return to the old ways.

—*Mary Eve*

PART TWO

Empowering the Power Parent

CHAPTER

5

Learning to Let Go

Four Responses That Never Work

- "Over my dead body."
- "Save it for marriage."
- "When I was your age . . ."
- "I don't care what everyone else's mother lets them do."

Responsophobia: The Fear of Getting it Wrong

Think back to the last time your teen said or did anything that shocked, surprised, disgusted and/or wounded you. Now try to recall what you were thinking one hour later:

- I was too lenient.
- I was too strict.
- I was too political.
- I was not political enough.
- I gave her too much responsibility.
- I was too protective.

If you thought any of these things, you have *responsophobia*, the completely rational fear of reacting at all to your teen.

Now, the Power Parent would *not think any of these things.* The Power Parent has only one response to everything her teen says or does: "Good for you." Yes, that's all there is to it!

Getting to "Good for You"

OK, it isn't as easy as it sounds. But after a few weeks of practice, you'll find that not only are you saying "Good for you," *you are believing it!* You will experience feelings of freedom that will not be matched until your teens leave home.

Example:

Your daughter, age 13, has found her first boyfriend. She says he is kind, smart, cute and likable. When you ask how old he is, she says he just turned 24. You say:

Wrong: He's old enough to date me.

Right: Good for you.

Example:

Your son's voice cracked during his solo in the gala spring concert, so now he's been in his bedroom for 10 days and refuses to come out. You say:

Wrong: Come out here, you little wimp.

Right: Good for you.

Example:

Your daughter withdrew her savings from the bank and blew all of the money on video games in 20 minutes. You say:

Wrong: Why didn't you just flush it down the toilet?

Right: Good for you.

Example:

Your 16-year-old son wears battle fatigues, shaves his head, subscribes to reactionary magazines and accuses you of living before he was born. You say:

Wrong: You are a fascist running dog of the imperialist military-industrial complex.

Right: Good for you.

Example:

Your son has joined a rock band called Pond Scum, which performs in clubs you are too old to get into, and has an act involving live banana slugs and rock salt. You say:

Wrong: Why can't you join Junior Achievers, like your cousin Ralphie?

Right: Good for you.

From Mary Eve's Mailbag

Dear Mary Eve:

A few days ago I noticed a peculiar odor emanating from my 14-year-old daughter's bedroom. I tried to let go, but today the smell was so foul I could not stop myself from entering her room. Imagine my surprise when I discovered two teenagers I had never seen before. They told me their parents didn't understand them and that my daughter had said they could live with us. Help!

—*Frantic* in Fresno

Dear Frantic:

Power Parenting is about trusting your own negligence. How long do you think your daughter will be happy in that room with two trapped adolescents? You don't have to do everything, you know. And by the way, what was that bad smell?

—*Mary Eve*

Example:

Your daughter tells you she is moving out on the weekend to join the Rainbeaux, a group of quasi-religious nomads who wear gray and drive up and down the West Coast worshipping rain clouds. You say:

Wrong: Why be born again?—surely once was enough.

Right: Good for you.

Example:

Your son's outfit for a visit to your extremely conservative parents: a leather jacket spray-painted with the words "Death Lust," torn blue jeans that reveal areas of his jockey shorts, and buttons that read "So What," "Who Cares," and "Up Yours." You say:

Wrong: I certainly hope your grandpa's papers are in order.

Right: Good for you.

Example:

Your daughter has become the Vegan Without a Cause. She refuses to eat at the table when animal products are served and she leaves provocative anti-vivisectionist literature on your pillow. You say:

Wrong: People who live on tofu eventually go blind.

Right: Good for you.

Example:

Your daughter is on her way out to meet a boy she found on the Parti-Wires, a public service that introduces strangers on the telephone. You say:

Wrong: Why don't you just get a T-shirt that says VICTIM on it?

Right: Good for you.

Getting to "Good for Me"

When you learn "Good for you," the big bonus is "Good for me." That is, "Good for you" transfers the burden of responsibility for your teens to the teens themselves, and you are free of it. The hours you used to spend crying, worrying and leaving messages on your doctor's answering machine, you can now spend playing golf, reading murder mysteries, going to Chant for Monetary Success workshops—whatever *you* like to do.

When you say "Good for you," believe it. Let yourself become absolutely self-centered. Let yourself be a Power Parent.

From Mary Eve's Mailbag

Dear Mary Eve:

My 15-year-old daughter got her high school yearbook signed by a number of chums who addressed her as "Ellie, you slut," "Dear Ellie, or should I say Blaze Starr," etc. Are these just teen jokes, or. . . ?

—*Aggrieved* in Grand Rapids

Dear Aggrieved:

Don't tell me you haven't any reading material more stimulating than a high school (yawn) yearbook!

—*Mary Eve*

Dear Mary Eve:

Last night my husband and I came home early from Bridge Club to find our 16-year-old son wearing my best dress! My husband said it looked better on him than it did on me. What do you think of that?

—*Furious* in Eugene

Dear Furious:

If that's what your husband thinks of that dress, why not give it to your son? Let go, Furious!

—*Mary Eve*

CHAPTER

6

Parent Throttling

Pre–Power Parents labor under twin illusions:

- It is possible to reason with teens about their feelings.
- It is desirable to reason with teens about their feelings.

"Reason" and "feelings" simply do not belong in the same sentence. Asking a hormone-crazed teen or a guilt-crazed parent to make sense of her feelings is like teaching a dog to read a book—it only brings humiliation upon both of you. Besides, when the experts say "reason with," they really mean "manipulate," which never works. Teens learn so fast that minutes after you begin "reasoning with" them, you'll be left in the dust, manipulationally speaking.

Example:

Bonnie, 16, has planned a glorious weekend. Friday after school she and her best friend will hang out at the mall. They will then go to the Cineplex with their boyfriends to see "Spread-Eagle Chicks: The Movie." All four teens will spend the night at Bonnie's friend's house (the friend's

mother is out of town). On Saturday afternoon Bonnie will come home, shower and dress in an outfit that includes Mother's suede boots. She will then go to a big party on the other side of town and take the last bus home, alone, at 1:00 a.m. On Sunday she will sleep all morning, sunbathe all afternoon, eat dinner and do a bit of homework.

In the old days, the communication process unfolded like this:

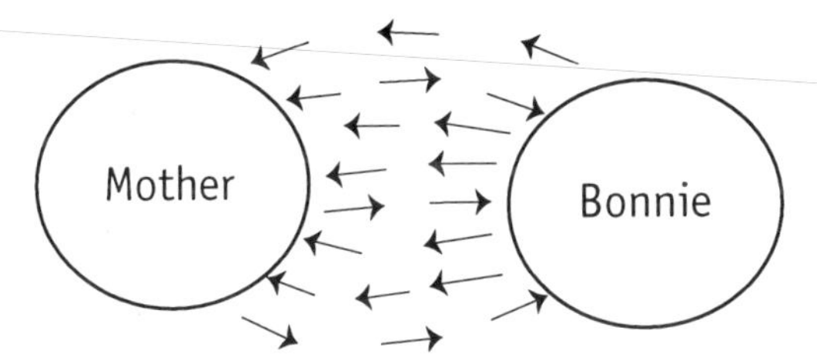

Mother: You WHAT? And WHAT? WHERE? (etc.)

Bonnie: You never want me to have any fun.

Mother: You and I have a contract about your household chores.

Bonnie: I have to do everything around here.

Mother: You and I have talked about misogynist pornography, haven't we, Bonnie?

Bonnie: You don't own me.

Mother: And don't I have a right to wear my suede boots on Saturday night?

Bonnie: Go ahead, ruin my outfit, I'll just wear something ugly.

Effective Parent Throttling (EPT)

Bonnie, a child of the 1980s, soon learns to decode Mother's feelings and make "I-statements" rather than "You-statements":

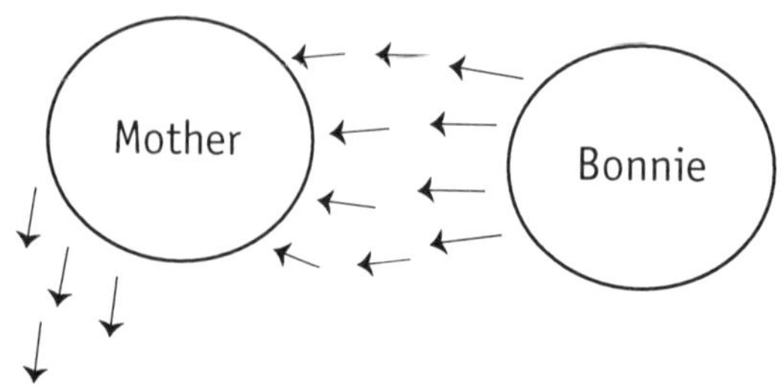

Mother: You WHAT? And WHAT? WHERE? (etc.)

Bonnie: I hear you being upset about many of my plans. Can we sort out your issues?

Mother: Um, my what?

Bonnie: I feel you are uncomfortable about me going to the Cineplex and not doing any housework.

Mother: Well, yes . . .

Bonnie: I imagine you are jealous that I look about 300% better in your suede boots than you do. You worry that I'll get pregnant or get a dose or a bad reputation if I sleep with my boyfriend.

Mother: Yes, all of that. But I want you to have fun.

Bonnie: Great! See you later, Mom.

The EPT dynamic allows Bonnie to be a Toxic Teen wrapped in the clothing of a mature, understanding person.

Affirmative Dynamic Effective Parent Throttling (ADEPT)

Similar to the EPT dynamic but even more insidious is ADEPT, in which Bonnie uses affirmation-like language to disable Mother's rage-anxiety matrix.

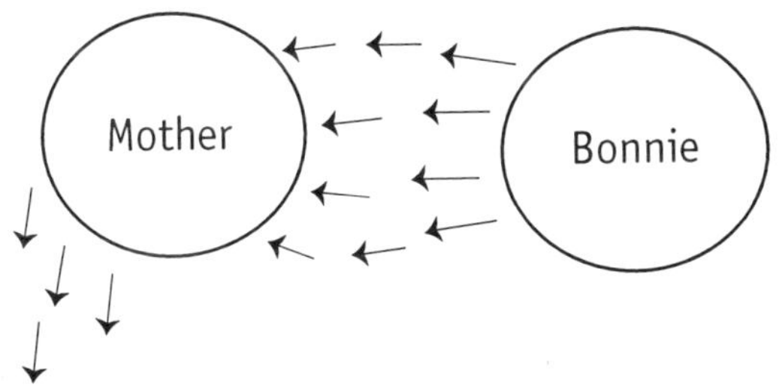

Mother: You WHAT? And WHAT? WHERE? (etc.)

Bonnie: I feel you are very worried and angry.

Mother: Of course I am.

Bonnie: It makes me feel so secure to have such a concerned mother!

Mother: (crying) Please don't stay overnight with your boyfriend.

Bonnie: That's great, Mom! Let it out!

Integrated Non-exclusive Effective Parent Throttling (INEPT)

Once they have fallen for EPT and ADEPT a few times, even pre–Power Parents are quick to move to INEPT:

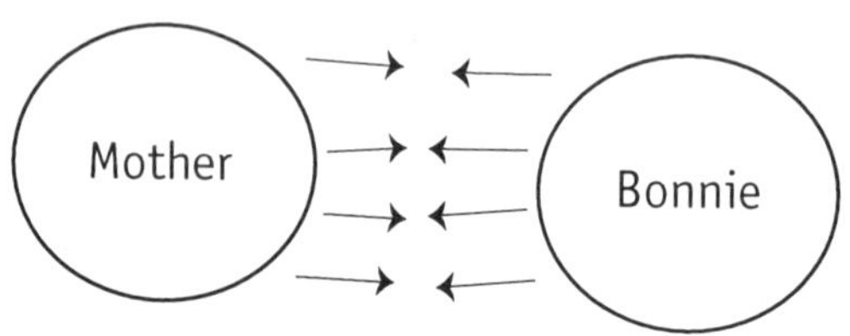

Mother: I know you're really looking forward to this weekend.

Bonnie: I feel you are very anxious about my plans.

Mother: I am very uncomfortable with some of the plans.

Bonnie: I am very uncomfortable with your discomfort.

Mother: The weekend you have planned just won't work for me.

Bonnie: The weekend you have planned just won't work for me.

Mother and Bonnie are locked in cross-manipulation for the rest of their lives, and they don't even get the satisfaction of hurling vicious insults at each other as they would in the old days.

Power Ratio Establishment for Counteracting Effective Parent Throttling (PRECEPT)

PRECEPT is the healthy Power-Parenting alternative to EPT, ADEPT, INEPT and all the other EPTs of the pesky me-first era. PRECEPT works because Power Parenting is not a matter of trickery or pseudo-democracy. It is a matter of letting go.

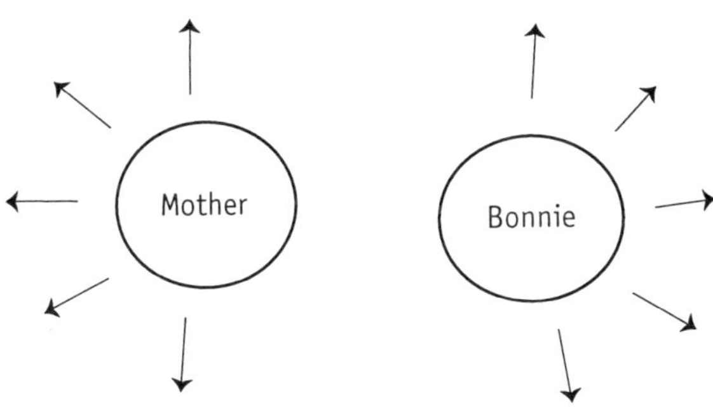

Mother: Good for you.

If PRECEPT seems scary, go deeper into your fears. What is the worst thing that can happen? Bonnie might be exposed to pornography, ruin Mother's suede boots, have sex with her boyfriend, and fail to do household chores for three days. All of this is going to happen anyway—if not this weekend, then some other weekend. Mother refuses to take it on, redirecting her energy to her own needs. She is calm and confident. She is a Power Parent.

CHAPTER

7

Teensactional Analysis

Let's look at it another way. Every exchange between ME (the parent) and YOU (the teen) is called a teensaction, and every teensaction is loaded—even thoughtless, innocent small talk. Over the years, the teensactions build into dynamics, most of them hopelessly sick.

Example:

> 15-year-old Marla wants to get a tattoo on her belly, a sprawling hearts-and-snakes extravaganza that features largely the name of her new boyfriend. What does Mother say?

1. Good for Me, Bad for You

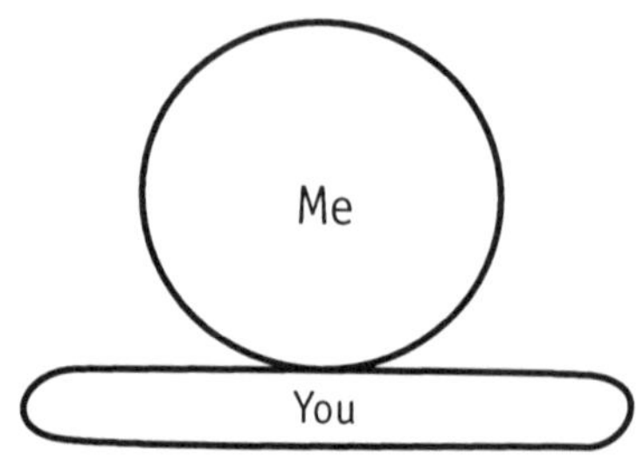

Mother contacts every tattoo parlor in a 50-mile radius and threatens to fire-bomb them if they touch her daughter. She launches a lawsuit against Marla's boyfriend, who, she is sure, dreamed up this preposterous plan. She reminds Marla that as long as she is under age 18, she can still be signed over to reform school.

2. Bad for Me, Good for You

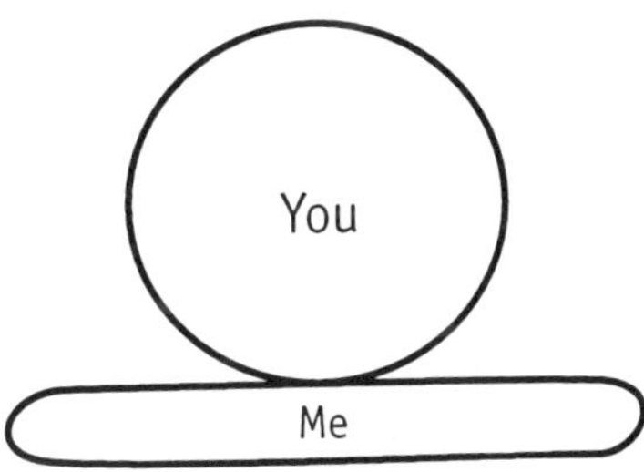

Mother lets Marla get her tattoo. In fact, she lends her the money to do it. Marla thinks Mother is the greatest. Mother knows that she has the backbone of a common garden slug. She also knows that although life is peaceful now, in six months Marla will turn on her, saying, "How could you let me disfigure my body with the name of that major loser!"

3. Bad for Me, Bad for You

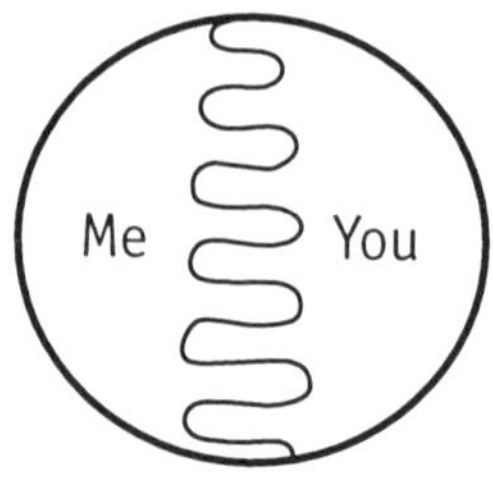

Mother accuses Marla of having sex with her boyfriend. Marla says, "If you can have sex with your boyfriend, I can have sex with mine." Mother reminds Marla that she was rude to her boyfriend the last time he came over. Marla says she learned rudeness by listening to Mother talk to her. Mother says Marla learned rudeness from that slut Angela she hangs out with, the one who made Marla's grades go from As to Cs in one semester. And so on.

4. Good for Me, Good for You

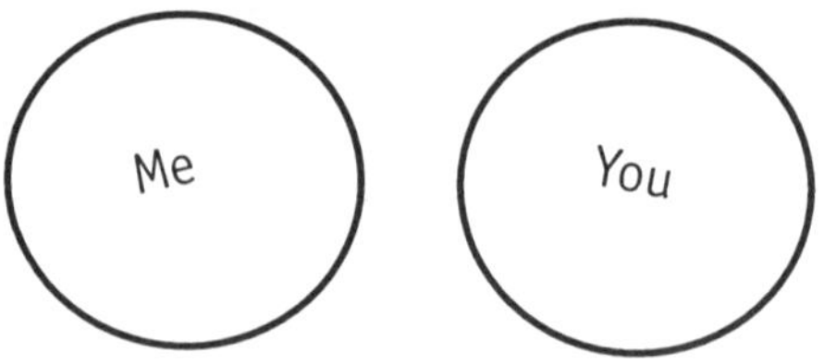

Mother can hear only part of what Marla tells her, because she's in a luxurious bubble bath, running the hot water. "Great, honey," she shouts at the door. "I'm glad you're over your phobia about needles. Pick up a head of lettuce on the way home, will you?"

Power Parenting Through the Ages

I admit here and now that I did not invent Power Parenting, I merely reclaimed the concept. The Power Parent has been with us since the beginning of time.

Ancient Moms

Also known as Metaphysical Moms, these parents sent their young adults off to the circus all day while they gathered in the city-states, learning how to think and how to write poetry.

Moms in the Middle Ages

Medieval Moms never worried about their teens, preferring to maintain a simple loving faith that everything would turn out all right. Privately they were thankful for the fall of Rome, which had been a bad influence on their adolescent children.

Renaissance Moms

Those who were not burned as witches declined to fuss about curfews and haircuts, as everyone was far too busy inventing the printing press and the landscape garden.

Reformation Moms

What with the Inquisition, the Counter Reformation, and creeping Calvinism, no one had time for acne or alienation.

Enlightenment Moms

The long tradition of Power Parenting began to falter with the emergence of Enlightenment Moms (not to be confused with modern Enlightened Moms, who falter so often they can hardly stand up). But then, anxiety about teenagers was bound to crop up in an age that favored reason, philosophy and conversation.

Industrial Moms

Snatching Power Parenting from the jaws of defeat, Industrial Moms put their teens to work in factories and sweatshops, leaving no question about who was in charge here.

Modern Moms

From the Roaring Moms of the '20s, the Depressive Moms of the '30s and the Patriot Moms of the '40s, came the Beatnik and Storybook Moms of the '50s and '60s. Postwar wealth made possible the phenomenon of the rec room, placing teens out of sight and, consequently, out of mind.

Postmodern Moms

'70s Hippie Moms wanted their teens to be free, if they knew which ones were theirs in the first place. Hippie Moms set the stage for '80s Punk Moms, who shocked the world by drying baby diapers for re-use (without washing them first) and out-teening their teens by sticking safety pins through their own noses and ears.

Power Parents

Making the empowerment choice in the face of relentless "expert" behavior-mod advice, these are the bravest parents in history, and a shining example for the parents of the future.

CHAPTER

8

Communicating with Teens

The Proof Is in the Mind-Mapping

By now you are ready to face facts. When either teen or parent says, "I hear where you're coming from," she is lying. You can prove this for yourself in a mind-mapping ("clustering") session with your own teen. Bribe her if you must to go through it with you. You choose a word or idea, then each of you charts her random musings on that word or idea.

Following is an actual example of a mind-mapping session. Parent and teen chose the word MONEY, then went into separate rooms and "clustered" independently for 10 minutes. The two resulting mind-maps follow.

Look carefully at these mind-maps.

- The money–food path for the parent is MONEY → FOOD → PLASTIC BAGS → GUILT, while the money–food path for the teen is MONEY → SPEND → RESTAURANTS.
- The teen mind-map displays no concern at all with such urgent money issues as HIGH

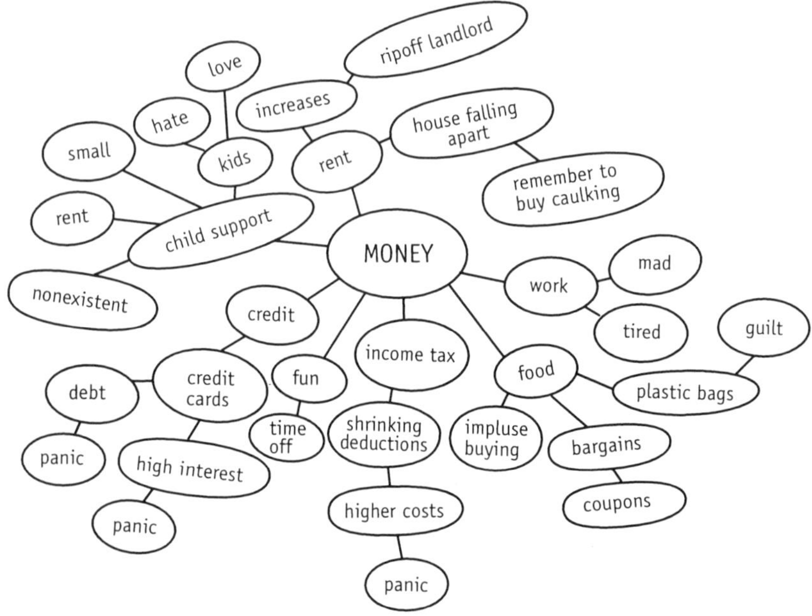

The Parent Mind-Map

INTEREST, CHILD SUPPORT, COUPONS or REMEMBER TO BUY CAULKING.

- Although both mind-maps display a loathing for paid employment, the parent mind-map path is MONEY → WORK → TIRED or MONEY → WORK → MAD, whereas the teen path is a breezy MONEY → JOB → HATE → QUIT.
- The only money-related destination parent and teen have in common is FUN. But for the parent, FUN connects with TIME OFF, while for the teen, FUN is associated with SNOWBOARDING.

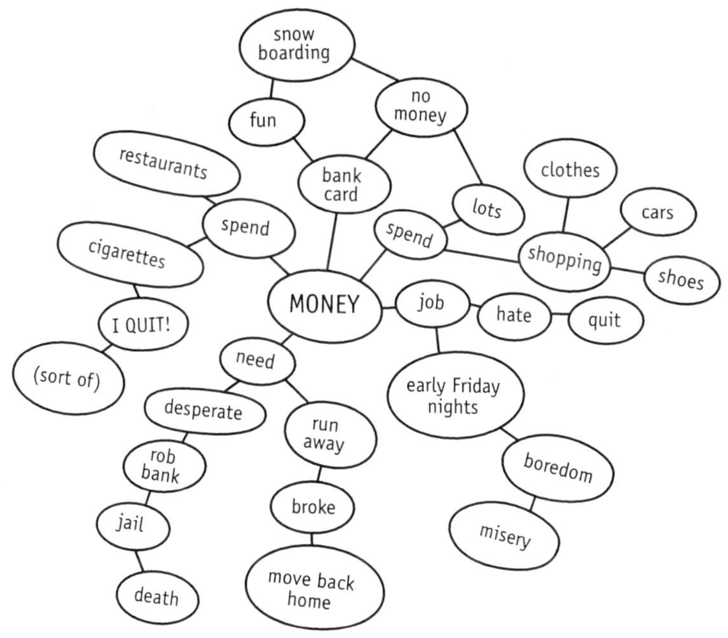

The Teen Mind-Map

Why Parents and Teenagers Cannot Talk

We all know parents of teenagers who make frequent and pathetic attempts to "keep the lines of communication open." To teens, this expression has to do with paying the monthly phone bill.

The fact is, words and expressions you take for granted have very different meanings for teens.

Word	Teen Definition	Parent Definition
Graduate	Fun-party-freedom	Drink-puke-screw
Sex	Fun-hot-forbidden	Exploitation-pregnancy-AIDS
Drugs	Fun-high-party	Sick-freakout-cops
Cars	Fun-fast-power	Crash-blood-cops
Sibling	Brat-swear-fight	Fun-secrets-support
Friend	Fun-secrets-support	Bad influence

Some words have even more complex meanings.

Sample Word: *Conversation*

Teen Boy	Teen Girl	Parent
Two guys grunting and cursing side by side at a hockey rink	Three or more girls all talking at once	Teen states opinion, parent corrects it

Sample Word: *Power*

Teen Boy	Teen Girl	Parent
Talking the most and loudest or driving the most and loudest or spending the most and loudest	Having the oldest boyfriend	Having the most trouble-free teens

When Talking Is Absolutely Necessary

Long periods of silence between parent and teen can be very positive. They have a healing effect because they eliminate the need for excessive worry. No news is good news, right?

However, there will be times when you simply *must talk to your teen*, and vice versa. What can you do?

Four approaches to talking that always fail:

- "How was school today?"
- "Let's share our feelings."
- "How was the party last night?"
- "You never talk to me."

Four approaches to talking that always succeed:

- "Don't you think it's about time you quit school?"
- "Here's $200—spend it on anything you want."
- "Got any hash?"
- "I have sold your baby sister."

The idea here is to get the conversational ball rolling by getting your teen's attention. Then all you need are the following easy techniques for getting through the actual talking period.

Non-adjudicational Monitoring

Incline your head toward your teen. Purse your lips and furrow your brow as though deeply pondering her words. Nod understandingly from time to time.

Example:

Judith has just come home from the movies and she needs to talk about it.

1. The pre–Power Parent conversation:

Judith: OK, so like there was this tall blonde, right, and—

Mother: Tall blonde *woman*, Judith.

Judith: And she has this boyfriend and he like really loves her, right, but then she like gets in this accident, right?

Mother: Stop saying "like" and "right" all the time!

Judith: OK, so like—I mean—OK so she, oh yeah but before that, I forgot, she like—oops, OK there was this other guy—

Mother: (yawning) Well, honey, it's past my bedtime.

Judith: OK, just forget it, you bag!

2. The Power Parent conversation:

Judith: OK so like the other guy, the first one, like he was really nice, right, but the blonde, like she only thought this other guy, Dave, no—Ron I think it was, like that he was the really cool one, only—no it wasn't Ron it was Dave, or was it Ron, OK so anyway but *before* the thing about the legs. You know what I mean?

Mother: Mm-hmm.

Non-lingual Messaging Interpretation

Decoding the unspoken language of adolescents is one of the great unsung arts. Start with these common examples, then build your own glossary.

What your teen does	What your teen is saying
Rolls eyes	Does she have to wear that gross sweater all the time?
Glances at watch	I'm missing *fifteensomething*.
Crosses and uncrosses legs	I wonder if my thighs look too fat when I do this.
Winces	I can't believe he still says "groovy."
Yawns	Sure hope I get a Nintendo for my birthday.
Refuses to eat breakfast	No way can I sit at a table with my family for ten whole minutes.

Caution: Sometimes the non-lingual messaging signal is not a cover-up:

What your teen does	What your teen is saying
Rolls eyes	This mascara is too thick.
Glances at watch	I wonder what time it is?
Crosses and uncrosses legs	I have to go to the bathroom.
Winces	Growing pains again.
Yawns	I'm tired.
Refuses to eat breakfast	I'm not hungry.

Storying

Storying means telling your teens anecdotes from your own adolescence. Sound silly? Not when you consider how your own teen years are portrayed in pop culture. Has anyone your age actually ever seen a beatnik wearing a beret and a pointy little beard, snapping his fingers and calling people "Daddy-O"? This is what our teens think we were like! No wonder they don't want to share their feelings with us.

So don't be shy. Tell them how you ran away from home at age 16 and lived for 3 months in your boyfriend's car before being caught. Or the time your parents went away for the weekend and you accidentally burned the house down. Or how you met your teens' father: a pay phone was ringing, you picked it up and the rest is history.

Avoid glamorizing these memoirs. Tell your teen how hard it is to bathe in a Chevrolet, how sad you were about the guitar you lost in the fire, what it was like to find out that you can get pregnant on a pay phone.

Teen Curfew Egg Chart

You don't have to break an egg if
you aren't going to make an omelette.

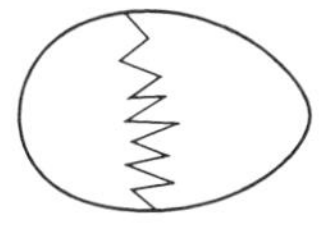

Your teen breaks curfew
once every 6 months.

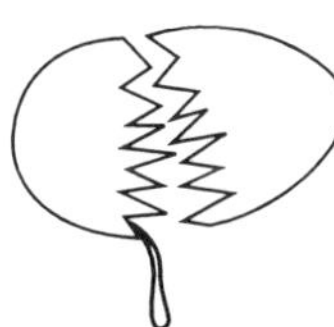

Your teen breaks curfew
once every month.

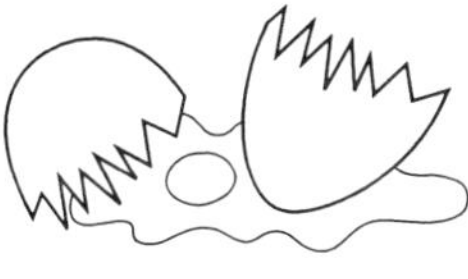

Your teen breaks curfew
once every day.

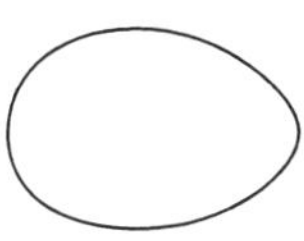

Your teen does not
have a curfew.

From Mary Eve's Mailbag

Dear Mary Eve:

Is it OK to smoke pot with my teenagers?

—*Perplexed* in Pensacola

Dear Perplexed:

Only if it's their pot.

—*Mary Eve*

Dear Mary Eve:

Recently my son came home from school and reported that he'd had sex education in his health class. The teacher was very open about everything, which was fine with me up to the part where he ate a handful of Delfen foam, "to prove it doesn't taste bad." What should I do?

—*Distraught* in Detroit

Dear Distraught:

Get that man's name and phone number and send it to me at once.

—*Mary Eve*

CHAPTER

9

Teen Health

When little kids are sick, they're sick. Alas, the ailments of teens are not so uncomplicated. Many an unwary parent has been drawn into a vortex of confusion, pity and suspicion when her teen is indisposed. This guide will save you hours of distress as you deal with teen maladies over the years. And remember, the guide is not meant as medical advice. When in doubt, call your family physician, if she is not avoiding you.

Common Teen Symptoms and Treatment

Symptom	Probable diagnosis	Treatment
Aural hypo-sensitivity (deafness)	Heavy metal music played on powerful Walkman	Stop talking to teen, she can't hear you anyway
Aural hyper-sensitivity (ability to hear any noise from long distances)	Really juicy argument going on in home	Postpone fight until teen goes out
Nausea	Recent overindulgence in pizza and/or beer	Ignore teen

Symptom	Probable diagnosis	Treatment
Bloodshot eyes	Recent overindulgence in violent Hollywood cop shows	Learn psychic numbing
Itchy scalp	Cheap hair dye *or* Under-bathing *or* Over-bathing *or* Head lice	Build private residence for teen
Other maladies	Various	Mind own business

Conditions that often require medical attention	Conditions that often do not require medical attention
Acne	Acne
Coughing	Coughing
Twitching	Twitching
Bleeding	Bleeding
Bones protruding from torn flesh	Bones protruding from torn flesh
Rashes	Rashes
Screaming in pain	Screaming in pain
Unconsciousness	Unconsciousness

Teen Maladies That Can Be Treated

The Power Parent recognizes the difference between injury/illness (see above), which is usually best treated with active neglect, and grotesque symptoms described by teens but invisible to anyone else:

Overbite
Underbite
Chin too pointy
Chin too round
Eyebrows too bushy
Eyebrows too sparse

Body too angular
Breasts too small
Breasts too large
Penis too small
Wrong shape rear end
Wrong color eyes

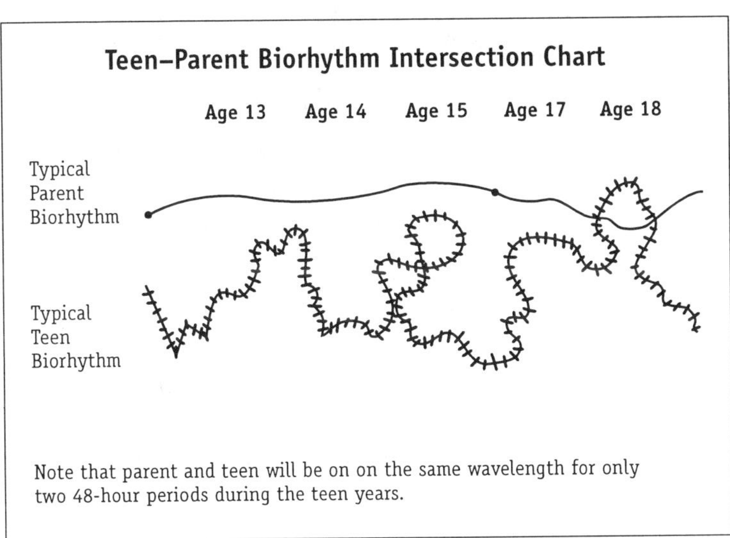

Nose too large
Nose too small
Adam's apple too big
Teeth crooked
Bowlegged
Knock-kneed
Early menstruation
Late menstruation
Body too short
Body too tall
Body too round
Wrong shape thighs
Voice too high
Voice too deep
Wrong shape fingernails
Wrong shape feet
Too much body hair
Not enough body hair
Lips too thin
Lips too full
Knees too bony
Knees too fleshy
Wrong color hair
Feelings too sad

Two simple home remedies are always effective for the complaints listed above: Belgian chocolate and cash.

CHAPTER

10

Timeless Paths of Power Parenting

All animals know how to parent. It is the most natural biological function in the universe. This is true and, in its way, beautiful. But remember: animals do not have teenagers. People do.

The New Age movement, with its blend of parapsychology, Eastern mysticism and capitalist fundamentalism, is a wonderful source of Power Parent techniques. The New Age guides the Power Parent to her rightful place in the universe—dead center.

Chanting for Power

The Power Parent strives for a tranquil, positive state of mind. Borrow liberally from Eastern-style meditation and get yourself a mantra—a word, phrase or prayer that you repeat many times while relaxing physically.

Example:

Your daughter drove your car into the tree behind the garage.

Example:

Your son was arrested for shoplifting at a department store full of warning signs, closed-circuit cameras and obvious plainclothes detectives.

Pull the shades, remove your shoes, lie down, close your eyes and say these words over and over and over again: "Good for me, good for you. Good for me, good for you. Good for me, good for you."

Parents report that this simple technique gives them a warm, fuzzy feeling of not caring about their teens at all. It makes them feel better instantly.

Power Visualization

Nothing causes more stress than living with teens. Scientists have proven that you can reduce stress with visualization, the art of mentally picturing your problem, then picturing how you want things to be.

Example:

17-year-old Chuck says he and 6 friends are going to drive 1500 miles to a rap music concert, in an open pick-up truck, in the middle of January. Father experiences crushing headache, bile rising to his throat, constricted breathing and an overwhelming sense of panic.

Father goes to his room, shuts his eyes and pictures the problem. In his mind's eye, Father reduces Chuck to a tiny mosquito, which he flicks away with his pinkie finger. Father has added 6 months to his life expectancy.

A short-cut to this method, the One-Minute Visualization, is described on page 66.

Pendulum Power and Parent Power

New Age practitioners draw shamelessly from ancient wisdom, so why shouldn't you? Try pendulumism, the art of handling a pendulum so that it reveals the energy fluctuations in any object—including your teen.

Example:

> Your family is enjoying a pleasant dinner until someone asks your 15-year-old daughter to pass the salt. She leaps out of her chair, knocks it over, screams "FIGHT THE POWER!" and stomps from the room. Everyone falls silent and sits wide-eyed and trembling.

When your daughter sits down to dinner, let the pendulum swing behind her back. Immediately you will know whether you will be dining with the Hopeless Monster (pendulum tends to the right), the Reasonable Human

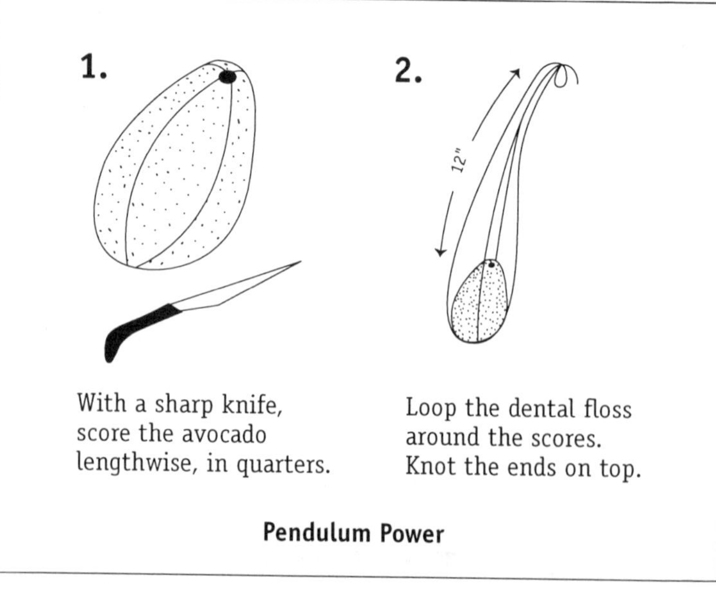

Pendulum Power

Being (pendulum swings to the left), the Tiny Baby (pendulum curls up), etc. If the pendulum is absolutely still, you should employ Non-lingual Messaging Interpretation (page 46); if it seems actually to rise in the air, try Power Parenting with the underside of the brain (*see below*); if you can't figure out what the pendulum is doing, just say, "Good for you" (page 24). Better yet, go out for dinner and leave her there with a frozen pizza.

The pendulum need not be a fancy store-bought model. Rig up your own with an avocado and a piece of dental floss.

Power Parenting with the Underside of the Brain

The right brain/left brain theory says that our brains are divided into two hemispheres: the left brain, home of logical thought, and the right brain, home of creativity and intuition. In parents of teenagers there is a third brain segment, the Underside of the Brain.

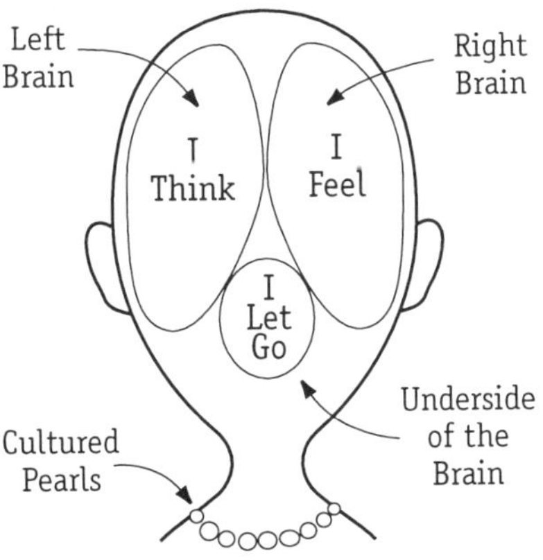

The Parent's Brain

The underside is chaos-controlled and filled with random particles. Left dormant, it just uses up space between your ears. But when it is activated, look out! Primal, powerful, fiendish Power Parenting solutions are released from the underside of the brain.

Example:

> 14-year-old Nathan is 5 feet tall and not growing. His friends tower over him, as does the shortest girl in his class. Nathan is apathetic and listless. His grades take a nose dive. He stops watching TV, bathing and, finally, going outdoors.

Father lies down in a darkened room and concentrates on his problem. Then he bounces the problem back and forth between his right brain and his left brain, logic to intuition, faster and faster until particle fission occurs and a brilliant, obvious solution emerges. He experiences this state as "white light," "hot" and "explosive." A week later, he goes on a TV game show and wins a complete home gym. Nathan is still 5 feet tall, but his new powerful body brings him respect, admiration and success among the ninth-graders.

Example:

> Laurie, 15, has a serious heavy metal music addiction. Day and night the sounds of Slayer and Iron Maiden throb through the tiny house. Mother cannot afford the ideal Power Parent solution—building a separate residence for Laurie. She is starting to lose it.

Mother practices Power Parenting from the underside of the brain, described above, and creates "Turn off Metallica–Turn on Mozart," one of our Subliminal Subversion Tapes (see Power Parent Enhancement Products, pages 78–80).

Now Mother and Laurie go about their business to the strains of gentle baroque music.

Self–Parenting and Self–Power Parenting

Many people have discovered that their own parents neglected them, and they are turning to self-parenting as a way to get mothered as they should have been in the first place. What a great solution for teens, who always hate their real parents!

Example:

> Naomi, 14, likes to spend money but refuses to accept jobs babysitting or delivering newspapers because they pay "zero money." She asks Father for a hefty allowance.

Father encourages Naomi to visualize the perfect parent and to turn to that inner parent whenever she needs it. Then he wisely does not contradict Naomi's self-parent. "Talk to the parent within," he tells her. "Think of me as the parent without." He goes out dancing.

Chaos Power Parenting

Chaos theory is the science of patterns of unpredictability. Parents of teenagers, and only parents of teenagers, understand this concept—that rational, safe, knowable facts are nothing but a complex set of both random and organized data.

Example:

> Your 16-year-old daughter is a whiz at calculus, but she thinks pregnancy is something that happens to other people.

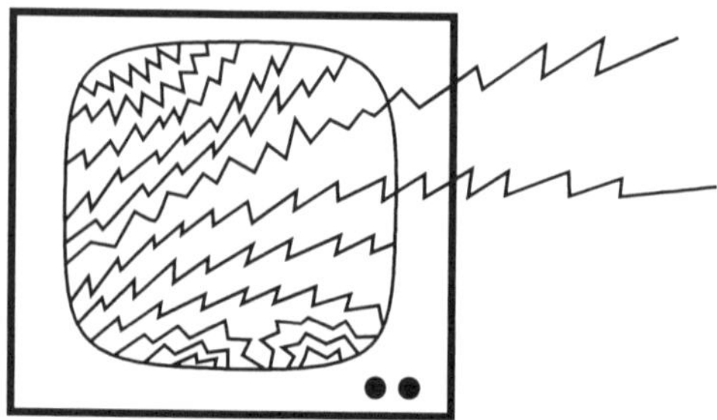

Chaos Power

Example:

Your 15-year-old son is a vegetarian and peace activist who beats the bejesus out of his younger brother once a month.

After years of expensive experiments, eminent chaos theorists have accepted the mysteries of the universe by arriving at the nucleus of Power Parenting: Don't say no, just let go.

Other New Realities

Channeling

Get in touch with James Dean, Buddy Holly or the teen angel of your choice. Let them speak through you, directly to your teen. Fortunately you, as the medium, won't even have to listen to the conversation.

Karmic Parenting

You reap what you sow. Give your teen the kind of Power Parents you wish you had, instead of the repressive, violent, abusive and otherwise "involved" parents you actually did have.

Zen Parenting (Less Is More)

What is the sound of one Power Parent ignoring her teen's choice of associates? Blissful silence.

From Mary Eve's Mailbag

Dear Mary Eve:

My daughter dyes her hair jet black every month, even though she has gorgeous natural red hair and the dye gives her severe allergic reactions, such as asthma and open running sores. I just can't stand to see her like this!

—*Broken* in Bridgeport

Dear Broken:

Then don't look.

—*Mary Eve*

Dear Mary Eve:

I was shocked the other day to discover my son and his friends lighting each other's farts. Surely this is not acceptable behavior for a young man!

—*Chagrined* in Chicago

Dear Chagrined:

Are you kidding? Did you ever hear of Robert Bly? Get a grip, Chagrined! Your son is sitting on a gold mine.

—*Mary Eve*

CHAPTER

11

Letting Go, Kicking Out & Living It Up

Most teens dream of leaving home. But some teens dream of staying home forever. I have met parents of 22, 25, even 27-year-old teenagers! When the Reasonable Human Being in your teen says, "Let's get the heck out of here" and the Tiny Baby drowns it out with a powerful, "And give up free room and board?" you need the Power Parenting method, even if you got by without it before.

Example:

Candice, 21, has flunked out of two colleges and lost three jobs since graduating from high school.

- **The pre–Power Parent sequence:** Mother calls a friend and persuades her to hire Candice. Candice goes to work. Mother collects rent. Candice quits her job. Mother persuades her to get re-hired. Candice quits her job. Mother gets Candice a student loan and admission into a college 2,000 miles away. Candice quits school and comes home. Mother introduces Candice to a nice boy at the plant. Candice falls in love with

the nice boy and moves in with him. The nice boy loses his job. He and Candice and their new baby move back in with Mother.

- **The Power Parent sequence:** Mother turns her home into a halfway house for recovering workaholics. Candice and family move out for good.

Example:

Richard does nothing but eat, sleep and watch TV.

- **The pre–Power Parent sequence:** Father sells the TV. Richard does nothing but eat and sleep. Father removes all food from the apartment and takes his meals at Helen's Grill. Richard does nothing but sleep. Father cuts a hole in the roof of Richard's bedroom, as if for a skylight, but never installs the skylight. Richard covers the hole with green garbage bags and does nothing but sleep. Father turns the apartment into a tourist attraction, charging visitors $3 ($2 unemployed) to observe a superannuated adolescent in his natural habitat. Richard does nothing but sleep. Father wakes Richard up and offers him a 1964 Oldsmobile and $400 in cash if he will leave. Richard goes back to sleep.

- **The Power Parent sequence:** Father gives notice and moves into a bachelor apartment. Richard is removed by the new tenants.

Important note: Do not jump the gun. Employ one of the Power Parenting methods only when you are sure your teen has passed through all six stages of leaving home:

The Six Stages of Leaving Home

Stage 1—the first time
Stage 2—the second time
Stage 3—the prepenultimate time
Stage 4—the penultimate time
Stage 5—the ultimate time
Stage 6—the return

From Mary Eve's Mailbag

Dear Mary Eve:

Why would a bright, attractive 14-year-old girl spend an entire summer in a windowless basement room, watching TV and eating taco chips?

—*Distressed* in Daytona

Dear Distressed:

Why would you notice, when you're at the beach all day with your pals?

—*Mary Eve*

Dear Mary Eve:

My wife and I went out of town last weekend. When we came home, the neighbors told us that our 17-year-old son had spent the entire time entertaining party-animal friends, with the help of our food, our liquor, our CDs and our bed. We need a new approach.

—*Indignant* in Indianapolis

Dear Indignant:

Wrong! You need new neighbors.

—*Mary Eve*

CHAPTER

12

The One-Minute Mother

One-Minute Motherhood is based on two assumptions:

- No teenager can listen to her parent for more than one minute;
- A mother should be able to assume absolute power over her teen in one minute or less per day.

Anyone—yes, anyone, even a father—can become a One-Minute Mother. With practice, you can replace 24 hours of desperate anxiety with 60 seconds of a simple, fun, effective exercise.

The One-Minute Affirmation

Don't say no. The Power Parent knows it is always easier to say yes, especially these days when positivity has become a sort of religion.

Examples:

Teen: My period is late.

Mother: I'm so glad you aren't sexually repressed.

Teen: I'm selling your washing machine and buying a dirt bike.

Mother: You are so unselfish! Any other boy would want to have both.

 The One-Minute Prioritization

Take 60 seconds a day to prioritize. Remind yourself of what really matters.

Example:

Your son has been caught smoking dope in a suburban shopping mall. His grades are slipping, he has let his hair grow down to his nose and a youth gang has been coming around asking for him.

What really matters:

- You just won $10 in the lottery.
- The world has not yet been destroyed by nuclear war.

Example:

Your daughter spent all her birthday money on a tape recorder, which she uses to record compromising conversations between her brother and his girlfriend. Then she blackmails them.

What really matters:

- You will not have to replace your car for at least another year.
- The weather is improving.

The One-Minute Visualization

Your imagination can be your best friend when it comes to your teen. Creative visualization works for winning athletes and it works for winning Power Parents.

Example:

> Picture your teen coming home from a day of honors classes and virtuous extracurriculars. She kisses your cheek and asks you for your opinion on important current events. After helping you prepare dinner, she eats enthusiastically but not sloppily. She then puts on a gorgeous outfit that she bought at a thrift store, and goes out with her boyfriend, who is her age but mature, smart and quite wealthy. She comes home before curfew with no hickeys on her neck.

The impressionable Power Parent is soothed and healed by this vision, and the more cynical Power Parent is so nauseated by it that she starts thinking her real-life teen ain't so bad after all.

The One-Minute Euphemism

You can talk yourself out of a teen-induced anxiety attack by taking 60 seconds to re-word the problem. After all, it is easier to manipulate yourself than to manipulate your teen. Don't be afraid to appropriate the language of psychologists, New Age therapists and common liars.

Examples:

> Wrong: Brent has spoken only 2 syllables in 3 years.
>
> Right: Brent has found his own quiet path to inner psycho-spiritual awareness.

Wrong: Susan has a police record longer than your arm.

Right: Susan is committed to personal freedom.

Wrong: Adam wets the bed.

Right: Adam is so in touch with the small child within himself.

Wrong: My teenagers are out of control.

Right: I have freed my family from its confining knots.

The One-Minute Duck-Backing

Just let go. Take as your role model the humble duck, which simply lets water, mud and sewage slide off its back.

Example:

Your son has spent 1½ hours locked in the bathroom, and has flushed the toilet six times.

Example:

Your daughter has fallen deeply in love with a 30-year-old married man who has promised to wait until she is 14 to have sex with her.

The Power Parent would not waste more than 1 minute on either of these events. Lie down, shut your eyes and breathe slowly and deeply for 60 seconds, picturing yourself on an Alaskan cruise. Or just go to the kitchen and make yourself a large hot fudge sundae.

Let it slide off, let it all slide off. You have nothing to lose but your own panic.

The One-Minute Guilt Trip

When all else fails, take back your power with this time-tested last-ditch method. It takes only 60 seconds a day to nail yourself to the cross.

Example:

> "Sure, honey, you take the car. The buses don't run after midnight but not many muggers will be out in the pouring rain, and anyway I've got to start getting used to this prosthesis."

Example:

> "Of course I can spare $20! You know, just the other day I heard that it costs $110,000 to raise a child to maturity—not including a university education."

PART THREE

Getting from Where You Are to Where You Wanted to Be in the First Place

CHAPTER

13

The Power Parenting Check-In

The road to Power Parenthood can be a rocky one. Some parents adapt to the practice of creative neglect as if they were born to it, flinging their guilt to the winds almost immediately. Others, the ones I call Process Freaks, need frequent concrete demonstrations of their progress and reassurance that they are not being irresponsible. For them, there is the Power Parenting Check-In.

Designed to help you quantify your pain, the Check-In will remind you that others have it even worse than you do. It will help you spot your own incremental gains and, in the last throes of pre–Power Parenting, it will even help remind you of simple facts, such as your own name.

Copy the questionnaire and fill it out once a week. Each time you do it, notice how you are changing—moving, as you will, through debilitating guilt and the desire for vengeance, to manic self-loathing and self-mockery, to teen-mockery and harsh bouts of uncontrollable laughter, to resignation and then acceptance. When you start forgetting to fill it out, or it begins to seem like just too much hassle, you will know that you are well on your way to Power Parenthood.

For The Last Seven Days:

My name has been: ______________________________

My teen's name has been: ______________________________

My age: __________ Age of my teen: __________

Number of disagreements between me and my teen: ______

% minor arguments (garbage not taken out, 30-min. showers): ______

% major arguments (live rats in bedroom, expulsion from school): ______

% physical confrontations without permanent injuries: ______

% physical confrontations with permanent injuries (specify):

____

____

____

% other (specify): ______________________________

____

____

Number of meals my teen ate at home: ______

Number of meals remaining (21 minus the above answer): ______

% eaten in a good home (estimate): ______

% eaten in a good restaurant (estimate): ______

% eaten in a bad home (estimate): ______

% eaten in a bad restaurant (estimate): ______

% consisting of cheezies, chips, pop, etc. (estimate): ______

% skipped altogether (estimate): ______

Amount of household food my teen consumed between meals: ______

____

Amount of household food my teen's friends consumed between meals:

____

Number of hours my teen spent in the bathroom: ______

Number of hours I spent in the bathroom: ______

Number of dollars my teen cadged off me: ______

Number of times the school counselor phoned to say s/he was "concerned": ______

Number of times the school counselor phoned to say s/he was "extremely concerned": ______

Number of times my teen referred to the school counselor as a "dick-head": ______

Number of times my teen changed hair style: ______

Number of times my teen changed hair color: ______

Number of new items of clothing my teen was seen wearing: ______

% purchased (estimate): ______

% borrowed (estimate): ______

% traded for something less valuable (estimate): ______

% traded for something more valuable (estimate): ______

% stolen from me (estimate): ______

% stolen from others (estimate): ______

Number of words spoken to me by my teen: ______

% pleasant: ______

% insufferably rude: ____

% inaudible: ____

Number of times my teen spent more than 1 hour lying on the bed listening to a rock'n'roll song over and over: ______

Number of hours my teen spent looking in the mirror: ______

Number of hours my teen spent perfecting a new signature: ______

Number of hours my teen spent on the telephone: ______

% gossip and backbiting (estimate): ______

% schoolwork (estimate): ______

% phone sex (estimate): ______

Number of times my teen said "OK, OK, don't have a cow, I'm hanging up": _______

Number of times my teen found fault with my hair style: _______

Number of times my teen found fault with my clothing: _______

Number of times my teen found fault with my political beliefs: _______

Number of times my teen found fault with my breath: _______

Number of times my teen found fault with something else I can't help (specify): _______________________________

____

____

Number of mildew-covered dishes found in my teen's room: _______

Number of mildew-covered socks found in my teen's room: _______

Number of times my teen was obviously bored: _______

Number of times my teen was obviously drugged: _______

Number of times my teen was obviously in trouble with the police: _______

Number of hours I spent in tears because of my teen: _______

Number of hours of sleep I lost because of my teen: _______

Number of excuses I made for my teen's unacceptable behavior: _______

Number of lies I told friends and family about how well my teen is doing: _______

Number of times I read my teen's diary, desperate to know what the heck was going on with him/her: _______

Amount of prescription drugs I had to consume to cope with my teen: _______

Amount of non-prescription drugs I had to consume to cope with my teen: _______

Number of times my teen ran away: _______

Number of times I ran away: _______

CHAPTER 14

The Power Parenting Bookshelf

Power Parenting is one great idea that takes many forms. As you become more proficient at the method, you may feel the need for further reassurance or new inspirations, tailored to your own individual lifestyle. Here are a few of my favorite books:

Five Minutes a Day for a Greener Parent-Teen Relationship
Bobbi Shrimp

Combining ecography and psychography, Shrimp offers 100 quick-fix plans to healthier home dynamics. Five-minute sessions include smudging (ritual burning of bits of your teen's hair), daydreamwork (similar to Creative Visualization), aromatherapy (learning to enjoy the odor of your teen's running shoes).

One Foot in Front of the Other
Tara Flaubert

A book of meditations and affirmations for the emerging Power Parent—one thought for each day of the year. March 8 entry: "Happy International Women's Day! The

ILGWU did not gain power by trying to understand the garment moguls so must you take your own power without trying to understand your teens."

Grief Relief
Richard Miyake, M.D.

The author proposes that the agony of parenting teens stems from your sadness over the loss of your tiny, dependent, manipulable babies. Though grieving is very fashionable these days, I wouldn't recommend this text except for its list of suggested grief-soothers: extended partying, profligate consumption of comfort foods, and multidirectional whining.

Teen Havens
Roberta Perroni

Here are scores of useful and well-illustrated tips on how to create a separate dwelling space for adolescents, whether you live in a sprawling mansion or a ghetto apartment. Includes complete instructions on turning unused crawl spaces into teen alcoves, winterizing ordinary nylon pup tents and sneaking around the building code to renovate the garage.

The Tao of Power Parenting
Swami Blotchidananda

The teen . . . the parent . . . the wind . . . the ocean . . . the car parts rusting in the back yard . . . all are one. You and your teen are infinite in space and time. You can't own your teen, your teen can't own you. When you don't push, your teen can't push back. And so on.

Shop for Transformation
Pépé Juarez de Catarina

Looking for a way to beat those teen-parenting doldrums? This comprehensive guide to escape-shopping covers everything from the well-planned weekend Mall of America excursion, to the emergency mental-health impulse-buying binge in your own neighborhood. Tours involve no unrecyclable plastic bags and no products tested on animals with cute faces.

The Goodness! Book of Teen Records
Smart Alec Goodness

Open this little booklet to any page for the most shocking and embarrassing true teen tales the authors could assemble—much worse than anything your teen will do. Examples: the mother who bought her 16-year-old son goods and services worth $46,577 to get him to go live with his father, the 17-year-old who invoked the Freedom of Information Act to get access to her mother's anguish-filled diaries, etc.

CHAPTER

15

Power Parenting Enhancement Products

One of the keys to becoming a true Power Parent is treating yourself extremely well and quite often. Look for these effective and comforting products in your neighborhood therapy boutique today.

Let It All Go Stereo Radio Headphones

This deluxe set, made of flexible state-of-the-art foam-padded plastic, allows you to block out all unwanted noise, such as the sound of your teens fighting with each other or telling you their vocational plans for the future. Radio included, which electronically scans for and scrambles all stations catering to teenagers.

Power Parenting Cheat Sheet

It is easy to forget the "Good for you" rule when your teen is standing in front of you blaming you for your haircut, her haircut, the bus schedule and world hunger. Slip the Cheat Sheet's comfortable elastic band around your arm, slide the vinyl-covered, tastefully lettered list of

keywords into your sleeve and you will never again be caught without the proper Power Parent response.

Power Parenting Audio Prompt

Designed for those situations where the Power Parenting Cheat Sheet is inconvenient (i.e. when you are at the beach or sound asleep), this tiny, ingenious device fits snugly around your ear. It is programmed to respond to your teen's voice with the whispered words, "Say 'Good for you.' "

Flux Ointment

This potent, soothing emollient was formulated for the transition periods of Power Parenthood. In the weeks when you are saying "Good for you" through clenched teeth because you don't quite believe it yet, Flux Ointment provides temporary relief from hemorrhoids. Later in your learning period, when you may occasionally find yourself swallowing your pride, Flux will ease the way.

Single-Malt, Double-Shot, Triple-Strength Whiskey Samplers

The quickies in this compact case, standing only 3" high, slide easily under any bed, even a postmodern futon. The perfect companions to moments of crisis, they are teen-proofed with digitized locks which can be opened only by punching in your Parent Identity Code.

Power Parenting Subliminal Subversion Tapes

Train your teens' brains the E-Z way with these motivational tapes, which speak to your teens' subconscious minds. After all, there's no point in talking to their conscious minds. Processed with ultra-sophisticated

equipment, the tapes play simultaneously with rock audio tapes, CDs, and any radio station. 35,000 subliminal messages per hour are embedded in teens' favorite music—but they are aware of no aural interference! Titles include: I Want to Clean My Room, I'm Going to Get a Job, I Want to Get My Hair Cut, I Want to Let My Hair Grow, I Can't Wait to Visit Grammy and Gramps, I'm Never Going to See That Boy Again, Let Me at That Pile of Dirty Dishes, Turn off Metallica—Turn on Mozart.

The Power Parenting Training Video

Seeing is believing! The producers have created dramatic re-enactments of hair-raising true-life problems and Power Parenting solutions in action: 14-year-old Patricia, who became a train-hopping rock band groupie; 17-year-old Ichabod, who infected his parents' business equipment with twenty different insidious computer viruses; Shannon, who at age 15 graduated from stealing cars to stealing airplanes. 82 minutes, Beta only (Power Parenting has been around a long, long time).

Index

A

acne, 51
ADEPT, 32
allowance, increase in, 58
analysis, teensactional, 35
animals, and parenting, 53
aromatherapy, 75
audio prompts, 79
aural hyper-sensitivity, 50
aural hypo-sensitivity, 50

B

bad for me, bad for you, 37
bad for me, good for you, 36
bags, yellow, under eyes, 3
bait, rising to, ix
bath, bubble, 37
battered parent within, 17
Belgian chocolate, 52
bleeding, 51
bloodshot eyes, 51
Blotchidananda, Swami, 76
Bly, Robert, 60
bones, 51
boyfriend, too old, 24
brandy, snifters of, 14
bribery, effects of, 14

C

capitalism, 53
cash, 52
de Catarina, Pépé Juarez, 77
causality, duplex, 19
causes, political, 3
cave paintings, 6
challenge or nightmare, viii
Chan, Dr., 18
channeling, 59
chaos power parenting, 58
cheat sheet, 78
Chevrolet, bathing in, 47
Clearasil, 3
clustering, 40
co-teening
- characteristics of, 12
- definition of, 12
- disease process of, 14
- healing process, 16
- levels of, 14

communication process, 30
confusion, vortex of, 50
conversation, definitions of, 43
coughing, 51
cults, 26

D

dating other adults, 4
daydreamwork, 75
Dean, James, 59
dialogic signals, 19
Diego, Dr., 18, 19
do the right thing, desire to, ix
doubt, fear and panic, constant, 12

E

emotional battering, 4
empowering the power parent, 21
enhancement products, 78
EPT, 31
evolution, adolescent, psycho-intellectual, of, 18

F

family
- duplex, 18
- extended, 18

feeling vs. reason, 29
fiendishness, 57
five parts
- acceptance of, 10
- emergence of, 8
- shifting proportions of, 9

Flaubert, Tara, 75
Flux Ointment, 79
friend, 43
fundamentalism, 53

G

Geist, Dr., 18, 19
good for me, bad for you, 35
good for me, good for you, 37
good for you, getting to, 24
Goodness, Smart Alec, 77
graduate, 43
grief relief, 76

H

hair
  dyeing of, 60
  length of, 65
  loss of, 4
headphones, let it all go stereo, 78
hearts, scarred, 3
hegemony, 19
Holly, Buddy, 59
home remedies, simple, 52

I

illusions, twin, 29
INEPT, 33
inflow-outflow diametric, 19

K

kicking out, 61

L

leaving home, six stages, the, 63
left brain / right brain, 56
less is more, 60
letting go, 61
  learning to, 23
liberation, 19, 24, 27
life decisions, ludicrous, ix
lifestyle, teen vs. parent, x
living it up, 61
lying, to doctor, 4

M

mall, hanging out at, 29
Mall of America, 77
mantra, 53
meditations, affirmations and, 75
memoirs, avoid glamorizing, 47
memory, socio-evolutionary, 18
mind-mapping, 40
Miyake, Richard, M.D., 76
mooning, 4
music, heavy metal, addiction to, 57
mysticism, 53

N

nausea, 50
neck, pain in, 18
New Age, the, 53
nightmare or challenge, viii
non-adjudicational monitoring, 44
non-lingual messaging interpretation, 46
nonconfrontation, supportive, ix

O

one-minute mother, the, 64
  affirmation technique, 64
  duck-backing technique, 67
  euphemism technique, 66
  guilt trip technique, 68
  prioritization technique, 65
  visualization technique, 66
out-teening the teen, 16

P

paradigm shift, 18
parameters, situational, 19
parapsychology, 53

parent blaming, 5
parent throttling
affirmative dynamic effective, 32
effective, 31
integrated non-exclusive effective, 33
power ratio establishment for counteracting, 34
parenting
karmic, 59
Zen, 60
parenting, self-, 58
parents, poisoned, 1
parlor, tattoo, 36
pay phone, getting pregnant on, 47
Perroni, Roberta, 76
phone bill, 42
phone-dating, 26
pick-up truck, 54
power
chanting for, 53
chaos, and, 58
definitions of, 43
pendulums and, 55
underside of the brain, and, 56
visualization, and, 54
Power parenting
experts in, viii, 18
history of, viii
prayer, 53
PRECEPT, 34
pregnancy, other people's problem, 58
process freaks, 71
psycho-gurus, 5
purpose in life, lack of, 16

R

rap music, 54
rashes, 51
reading, further, 75
reality check, 12
reason vs. feeling, 29
relationships, adult, ix
repercussions, phenomenological, 18
responsophobia, 23
Rick, guy named, 4
rides, to Mexico, 4
right brain / left brain, 56

S

samplers, whiskey, 79
scalp, itchy, 51
school
flunking, ix
quitting, ix
self-centered, absolutely, 27
self-parenting, 58
sex, 37, 43
shoplifting, 54
shopping therapy, 77
short-shorts, spandex, 4
Shrimp, Bobbi, 75
sibling, 43
Sidhu, Dr., 18, 19
silence, blissful, 60
smudging, 75
sphere, relational, 19
storying, 47
subjugation, 19
subliminal tapes, 79
symptoms, physical and psychic, 3

T

talking
  approaches to, 44
  impossiblity of, 42
  when absolutely necessary, 44
tattoos, 36
teen
  age 14, 9
  age 18, 10
  Committed Social Worker, 8
  communicating with, 40
  five parts of, 7
  freeze-drying of, 19
  health of, 50
  Hopeless Monster, 8, 9
  impossible to live with, 19
  isolation of, 76
  leaving home, 61
  Reasonable Human Being, 8, 9
  refusal to clean room, 8
  staying home, 61
  staying out late, 8
  Tiny Baby, 8
  toxic, 1
  within (do without), 16
  World-Weary Existentialist, 8, 9
  wrong body for, 51
teen toxicity
  causes of, 5
  possibility of cure, 6
  symptoms, 6
  understanding, 7
teen-referencing, 12
teensaction, definition of, 35
therapy boutique, 78
things wrong, with body, 51
Tourette's Syndrome, 16
toxic tots, yesterday's, 5
twitching, 51

U

unconsciousness, 51
unspoken language, decoding of, 46

V

vegetarianism, 26, 59
video games, 24
video, the, 80
voice change, 24

W

war fantasies, 25
warfare, gang, 3
whining, multi-directional, 76
whole teen approach, the, 10